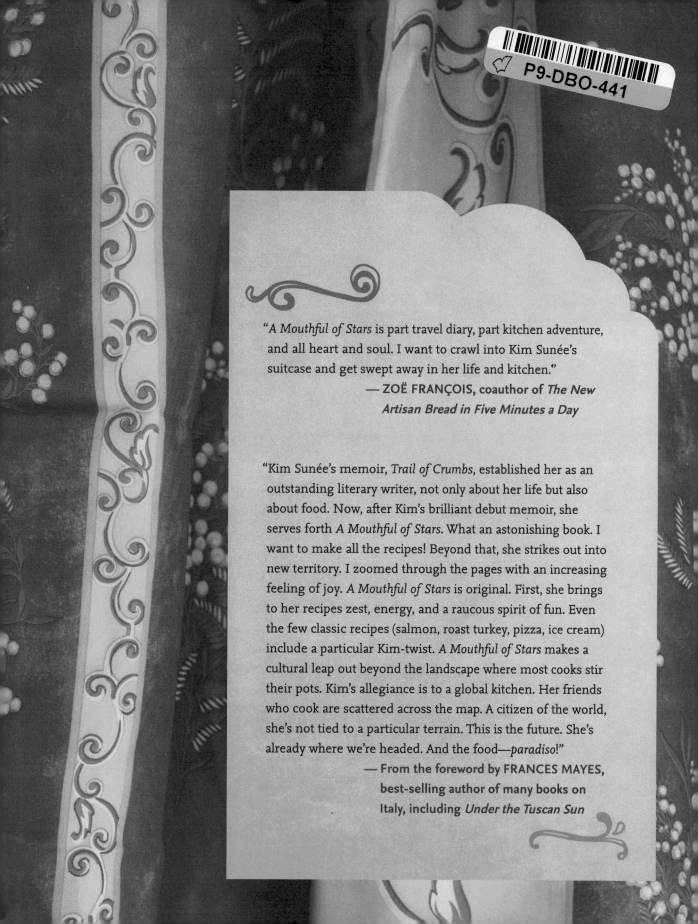

"A *Mouthful of Stars* is part travel diary, part kitchen adventure, and all heart and soul. I want to crawl into Kim Sunée's suitcase and get swept away in her life and kitchen."

— ZOË FRANÇOIS, coauthor of *The New Artisan Bread in Five Minutes a Day*

"Kim Sunée's memoir, *Trail of Crumbs*, established her as an outstanding literary writer, not only about her life but also about food. Now, after Kim's brilliant debut memoir, she serves forth *A Mouthful of Stars*. What an astonishing book. I want to make all the recipes! Beyond that, she strikes out into new territory. I zoomed through the pages with an increasing feeling of joy. *A Mouthful of Stars* is original. First, she brings to her recipes zest, energy, and a raucous spirit of fun. Even the few classic recipes (salmon, roast turkey, pizza, ice cream) include a particular Kim-twist. *A Mouthful of Stars* makes a cultural leap out beyond the landscape where most cooks stir their pots. Kim's allegiance is to a global kitchen. Her friends who cook are scattered across the map. A citizen of the world, she's not tied to a particular terrain. This is the future. She's already where we're headed. And the food—*paradiso*!"

— From the foreword by FRANCES MAYES, best-selling author of many books on Italy, including *Under the Tuscan Sun*

a mouthful of stars

ALSO BY KIM SUNÉE:

TRAIL OF CRUMBS: HUNGER, LOVE, AND THE SEARCH FOR HOME

a mouthful of stars

a constellation of favorite recipes
from my world travels

KIM SUNÉE

FOREWORD BY FRANCES MAYES

PHOTOGRAPHY BY LEELA CYD

Andrews McMeel
Publishing®

Kansas City • Sydney • London

for neil and liam
and for suzy

and all my fellow adoptees,
knee deep in stars and searching
for a taste of home . . .

Andrews McMeel Publishing, LLC, an Andrews McMeel Universal
company, 1130 Walnut Street, Kansas City, Missouri 64106.

www.andrewsmcmeel.com

14 15 16 17 18 WKT 10 9 8 7 6 5 4 3 2 1

ISBN: 978-1-4494-3008-5

Library of Congress Control Number: 2013952507

Design: Diane Marsh

Photography: Leela Cyd; except: Charlotte Brady: 114, 124-125;
Roberto Frankenberg: x, 168 (bottom left), 170, 216; Kim Sunée: xii,
xiii, xiv, 2, 4–5, 6–8, 17, 22, 28, 40, 49, 53, 55, 60, 62, 90 (except middle
left), 92, 96, 100, 119, 132, 151, 153, 154, 166, 168, 173, 174, 185, 191, 204,
215; Sara Essex: 59; Thayer Allyson Gowdy: 52; Valéry Trillaud: 64,
66, 81; iStock, 1, 27, 61, 115, 130, 131, 167

Food Stylist: Adrian J. S. Hale

ATTENTION: SCHOOLS AND BUSINESSES
Andrews McMeel books are available at quantity discounts with
bulk purchase for educational, business, or sales promotional use.
For information, please e-mail the Andrews McMeel Special Sales
Department: specialsales@amuniversal.com.

contents

acknowledgments

A VERY HEARTFELT THANKS to Joy Tutela and her colleagues at the David Black Agency who have been with me every step of the way, from crumbs to stars . . .

Grazie mille to the generous and gracious Frances Mayes, who was so kind from the very first cappuccino in Durham to those lovely days in Cortona with Ed and company cooking all day and later sipping wine under the star-studded skies.

For helping me see the constellation for the stars, thank you to the hardworking and lovely Jean Lucas for her steady hand in guiding and encouraging me to connect the dots. Also at Andrews McMeel, thanks so much to Kirsty Melville, Tim Lynch, Diane Marsh, Valerie Cimino, Dave Shaw, and Carol Coe.

Thank you to Scott Jones, who somehow during a trip to Chile sensed that the amazing Leela Cyd and I would make a great team. Thanks to Leela for her genius intuition in breathing life into these pages. And an enormous thanks to Adrian J. S. Hale for her careful edits and kitchen wizardry in making the food come to life.

Thank you for generously contributing photos from around the world: the breathtakingly talented Roberto Frankenberg in Paris, who happily accompanied me in Italy for "just one more bite"; the fun and exuberant Thayer Allison Gowdy in San Francisco; my sister from another life, Charlotte Brady; and the amazing Valéry Trillaud, from Paris to Cayenne and back.

No cookbook is complete without careful recipe testing and tasting. Special thanks to the wise and wonderful Laurie Constantino and Jennifer McGovern. Thanks to Sue Wiltse, who got me started, and to Chad Haynes, who kept me on track; to Christa Montgomery, Daniel Schumacher, Bob Thweatt, Julie Perilla, Kelli Parisian and Jeffrey Kendall, Bill Tierney, Sabrina and Chris Hargrave, Patrice Parker, Cat Lamb, and the Berg Family, especially Carrie and that wondrous palate of yours! Thanks to Rachel, Josh, and Jimmy for always wanting to eat more. With love to the Keim family—thanks for letting me mess up your kitchen so many times—and to Suzy, Joshua, and my parents.

Thank you to Adolfo Garcia, Sara Foster, Suvir Saran, Charlie Burd, Frank Brigtsen, Bill Smith, Jared Ralls, Jean Anderson, Martha Rose Shulman, Hugh Acheson, Zoë François, and Heong Soon Park. And to Stephanie and Joe Bischoff, Cindy, and Daddy Joe for always being ready to eat with me.

Thanks to Ivan Italiani for showing me how to make pizza and pasta. And thanks to Hongseok Ro (a.k.a. Roy) and Seung-Hee Lee, who showed me their country as if it were my own. Special thanks to Lee Herrick for taking my hand in our continued search for identity, and to James Schwartz for his friendship and on-the-spot editing genius; to Dr. John Floyd for teaching me so much about Southern cuisine; to Dr. Weir, for everything; and in loving memory of Dr. Grignon.

Thanks to Patsy, Paul, and Zoey (the best sister-in-law ever), and to Jan, my Parisian-Ohio sister. To Liam, such a fun chef-in-training, thanks for making me take breaks to play with light sabers and build Legos, and for reminding me of the merits of a simple grilled cheese sandwich.

And my love and thanks to Neil for building our nest and never wavering in his steadfast belief that I am home.

foreword

BY FRANCES MAYES

KIM SUNÉE'S MEMOIR, *TRAIL OF CRUMBS*, introduced me to a woman who'd had more adventures by age thirty than many have in a lifetime. From mysterious origins in Korea to a girlhood in New Orleans to a sojourn in Sweden and a rich decade in France—where she lived in sensuous Provence and later owned a poetry bookstore in Paris—this peripatetic girl is open to the wide world. Along the way, she acquired languages with her knife skills, many friends who cook, and a discerning palate. No one I know is more willing to hold out her plate and try—just try—whatever tasty morsel someone serves. She must have a million air miles, because the savory aromas of kimchi, Cuban pork, flying pasta soup, jambalaya, and blanquette de veau waft from across the globe and pull her to the airport. She returns with a suitcase jammed with exquisite chocolates, exotic pastes and jellies, Key limes, salsa—whatever temptations the markets offered. "I had heard," she writes, "that in the small historic village of Dolores Hidalgo, in the Guanajuato Mountains, two brothers sell unique ice-cream combinations in the plaza principal. With flavors such as mole, chicharrón, tequila, and pulque, I had to meet them." Later she experiments with the brothers' avocado ice cream, upping the ante with a bit of almond. Clearly, she is going to taste this world and continue to write about her experiences.

Trail of Crumbs established Kim as an outstanding literary writer, not only about her life but also about food. For her, food is "much more than sustenance." Her sense of a flavor remains inextricable from context. How fully she knows that the burnished brown loaf pulled out of a wood oven in France would not taste the same anywhere else, especially since the wine comes from the same earth as the wheat, and the neighbors who were born on that terra firma have gathered around the table. She knows the loaf personifies the very word bread.

Now, after Kim's brilliant debut memoir, she serves forth *A Mouthful of Stars*. What an astonishing book. I want to make all the recipes! She brings forward her early realization that food is place, food means the company we keep, food is comfort and home; all this, yes—assumed. Beyond that, she strikes out into new territory. I zoomed through the pages with an increasing feeling of joy. *A Mouthful of Stars* is original. First, she brings to her recipes zest, energy, and a raucous spirit of fun. Chapters are named not the usual vegetables, desserts, meats, and so on, but Fig of My Imagination, To the Moon and Back, and An Orphan's Thanksgiving— marking occasions of conviviality or, sometimes, solitude.

Second, she praises, philosophizes, and celebrates: This is our birthright, food that can be "relished with abandon." The bright balloons are released to soar, not held taut by their strings. Where many cookbooks stick to their serious purpose, Kim's aim seems to be to cook as she lives, passionately and expansively. She knows that "life isn't worth living without friends who know how to eat the heart out of a taco." This sensibility infuses every bite. How could I help but dash to the kitchen to try Grilled Peaches Wrapped in Prosciutto (page 174), Pan-Fried Peppers with Coconut and Tamarind (page 35), Salad of Roasted Cherries with Burrata (page 181), and Quick Pickled Fennel (page 13)? I love her delicate balance of flavors and aromas. Is she alchemist, conjurer, poet, or cook? All of the above. Even the few classic recipes (salmon, roast turkey, pizza, ice cream) include a particular Kim-twist.

I've said this is original, but let me take this idea where it wants to go. *A Mouthful of Stars* makes a cultural leap out beyond the landscape where most cooks stir their pots. Kim's allegiance is to a global kitchen. Her friends who cook are scattered across the map. A citizen of the world, she's not tied to a particular terrain. This is the future. She's already where we're headed. And the food—*paradiso*!

"the discovery of a new dish does more for the happiness of the human race than the discovery of a star."

—JEAN ANTHELME BRILLAT-SAVARIN

INTRODUCTION:
stardust memories

FOR YEARS, SEOUL WAS A CITY I understood to be part of my past, although with very few clues as to my birth family and how I ended up at the Star of the Sea orphanage. When I returned in 2008, it had been thirty-five years since I was considered a child of this country, lost at a marketplace, left behind by a mother I can hardly recall yet who remains an elusive and fascinating myth. Thirty-five years since I was adopted by an American family and recounted my memories, even at the age of three or four—of having a brother; the dance of sturdy women carrying fruit on their heads; the sparsely furnished house built off the ground with a spot heated from underneath where I'd wait in line to warm myself. And I would tell my American grandmother that the scent of overripe pineapple that was coming from her refrigerator drawer reminded me so much, somehow, of Korea.

In my first book, *Trail of Crumbs*, I wrote about these early beginnings; and about how they later informed my twenties, as I searched for a place to call home, mainly in France with an older, wiser, and grounded man who knew his place in the world, yet whose abundant love and money would not be enough to keep me from continuing the search.

So Seoul, like Paris and New York, Cayenne and Chianti, whirled past my fingertips on a spinning globe. How could I have known as a young girl in the humid, below sea level haze of New Orleans that I would leave in my late teens to study in Europe, and would soon rarely be without a passport, boarding pass, notebook, and camera? And that I would one day travel to and hunger after places like Cadaqués and Hong Kong, leaving parts of my self in French Guiana and Sweden, shards of my heart in Provence and Tuscany? I ended up traveling quite a bit; always, it seems in retrospect, longing for a taste of home.

Years later, and throughout my travels, I will have conversations with my younger sister, also adopted from Korea—although we are not blood related—about our early beginnings. It will pain me to hear her—the more grounded and reasonable of us—sigh as she asks, almost in a whisper, "Do you think we can find someone? Can we really find someone who lost us so many years ago?"

I always wish I could tell her something definitive and reassuring; that all we have to do is close our eyes and wish, that if we click our heels together three times then home will have a meaning. Although I misplaced my ruby slippers long ago, I still go forth like a pioneer and navigate the territory so I can report back to her and the many others who, like myself, are still wondering, and have written to tell me that they, too, may want to seek out their birth families.

I travel with no idea of who or what I will find, but I am always compelled to go. Travel for me is about the search and the people I will encounter along the way, the flavors and the places explored. Over the years, I've come to understand that being an orphan, being lost, may be where I started, but it doesn't have to define me for the rest of my life.

And because I've been grateful for every mile and every bite along the journey, one way for me to honor and return to these places, if not always physically, is through the evocation of meals, cooking and offering them to my friends and family.

The recipes I've gathered here are a collection of foods and combinations of flavors that satisfy in a deep-belly kind of way, and that together are more about fulfilling our basic needs and metaphorical hungers than replicating an exact technique or specific measurements.

The title of this book does not refer to the absolute most amazing dishes ever; rather, these are foods that I have experienced and loved and cooked and shared or that remind me of certain moments that stand out, like bright points of light—shining stars to help me navigate and connect the dots of a factless history of the self.

One bite of Pork Belly Korean-Style BBQ (page 14) brings back my most recent return journey to Korea and the amazing people and food I discovered there. Every time I suffer "roux wrist" from a hard-won gumbo or spike dirty rice with ground cayenne pepper,

I am honoring my New Orleans grandfather, Poppy, who as a thrifty cook was an example of how much simple joy there is in feeding others. And transforming flour and water into ribbons of pasta or steeping fresh lavender in simple syrup evokes many hours spent eating and cooking in Italy and the decade I spent in Provence and Paris.

I've cooked in many countries and kitchens around the world and yet often felt reluctant to call a single place "home." Although I've picked up languages and a certain kitchen patois, in particular, permanence in any form was never part of my vocabulary.

Perhaps this is one reason why my return to South Korea and to these other places that have marked me is worth contemplating: in order to understand something about my past that will allow me to conceive of a future in which I am not so alone. I have learned that through

chance meetings and the food we share, we instantly (albeit momentarily) can feel at home; the power of one bite can anchor us to a place and its people. So in many ways, this is a book about how we temporarily belong, through small but significant moments, mostly through travel and at the table. There's power and magic in food; it's enchanting to return to the same places expecting a taste of the familiar and discover something unexpected instead. There's joy and empowerment in becoming a better cook from having made each new discovery, and in being able to transform people, flavors, and places encountered along the way into something unique and delicious in one's own kitchen.

And, as I remind people who ask why all the care and time spent toward preparing a meal, I have this to say: We have to eat, so why not make the act thoughtful and deliberate? Because through these acts and shared moments, perhaps we will find our peace and our place in the world; and we might learn to nurture and nourish ourselves in such a way that will enable us to better tend to others.

As for stars, they are discoverable throughout nature. Cut an apple in half crosswise; look at an anise pod, a slice of carambola, pumpkin blossoms, lilies . . . from the sky to the sea and on the tongues of Benedictine monks who thought the Champagne they were drinking was stars. A friend wrote to me once, "Sometimes I think that we adopted people live our lives knee deep in stars." When I asked him if his own book about wine was also about adoption, he said no, but that only an adoptee could have written it. I feel

that way about both *Trail of Crumbs* and *A Mouthful of Stars*.

It makes me think of the great M. F. K. Fisher, who once wrote that when we write about food, we are also writing about love. So, in many ways, food is never just about food, is it? Lunch is never just lunch. And supper is more than the sum of its parts. And so, as we travel and cook and share the gifts of the table, we are also wondering, imagining, answering and asking questions of ourselves and of one another.

Looking back on when I was in my twenties and dizzy with airport codes and boarding passes to Venice, Athens, Tunis, and elsewhere, I realize now that I was in such a hurry, for everything, for life to be richer and deeper and for love to make sense and yet, underlying it all was the steady heartbeat of self-doubt. How dare I ask to be loved so much? How dare I wish to love? As a young child abandoned on the other side of the world, I sensed the answer was that I would never deserve it.

Chronicling what I've tasted, observed, and loved, *A Mouthful of Stars* reveals the inspiration and narratives behind my favorite recipes, some of which also parallel my emotional journey from single girl and restless traveler to fearless cook with a kitchen to call home. *A Mouthful of Stars* honors the flavors that root us to a place and to its people, because I have learned that no matter how far we roam, food can always give us a sense of home.

seoul

CHAPTER ONE

silkworms, flying pasta, *and* two-two fried chicken

I'M SITTING IN THE SEVENTEENTH floor club-level lounge of the Grand Hyatt Seoul. The hotel, with its deep waterfalls and spa, is a calming refuge built high on Mount Namsan, overlooking the bustling streets of the Itaewon district just below and the Han River beyond. I wonder, of the 10 million people in this city, is there anyone out there who remembers me—who knows my true birth date or recalls the first word I ever pronounced?

Since my arrival back in Seoul, I've been the first guest in the club lounge for breakfast, as it has been difficult to sleep for more than three hours a night with jet lag and the sheer emotional exhaustion of being back in this city. I am here not only for the Korean language edition of *Trail of Crumbs* but also because Roy, a Korean filmmaker who studied film at UC Santa Cruz, has been documenting my visit as an orphan returning home. I am fortifying myself now with lightly smoked salmon, toast, pumpkin porridge, and Solomon's root tea—a nutty, woodsy aromatic that I have come to associate with early mornings here in Korea.

In a few hours, Roy is coming to pick me up to tour the city, which I hope includes eating; I am craving the flavors of Korean street food. Even during my first brief and disquieting return journey in 1994, I found the food wholly satisfying; fulfilling in many ways that the country and people were not at the time.

"Soon-ay," he calls me in a rush, hugging me close; he has become a brother and Sherlock Holmes in this mystery we are trying to unravel. "We must return to the market where you may have been abandoned. I have Mike, my translator, here to come with us." He explains that after some investigating, he and Mike decided we should visit Sinpo Market since it is the only one near the Star of the Sea orphanage—the only concrete place noted on my adoption papers.

I've asked my new friend Lee Herrick, a poet who lives in California, to accompany me on this excursion. Lee and I corresponded for months before meeting on the first evening of my arrival in this country—where we were both born and both abandoned.

As we arrive in the port city of Incheon, I am reminded how much port cities have always fascinated me, with their ships and promise of new cargo; the temporary feeling of being anchored; the illusion that we are moored.

When the camera starts rolling, Lee and I, taking some long-forgotten, subconscious cue, follow the trail from one end of the market to the other. We are a makeshift Hansel and Gretel lost in a bazaar instead of a wilderness, making our way through the fish and vegetable stalls, tasting everything we can along the way: gumbo-like stews, steamed pork buns, and rice cakes in a sweet and spicy red sauce thick as blood. The elders of the area offer to help, scribbling maps of where to go, and offering advice on how best to find the way home.

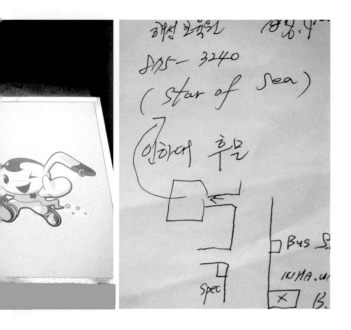

A few days after the visit to the market, Roy, who has spent thirty-six hours editing, calls to say he is coming to the hotel to watch the documentary debut nationwide with me and my new friends, interpreters Won and Seung-Hee.

"Soon-ay," Roy says, before hanging up, "I have to tell you something. Someone who thinks he is your brother is coming, too. No worries. He has a real job, is a nice man, and wants to meet you."

Roy goes on to explain that the man, Dong-Il, is vice-president of a company that lends ships to port cities around the world, and that he had originally planned on meeting me the day I was scheduled to appear on a show called *I Miss You*, where orphans try to reunite with their birth families. Since my appearance was postponed, Dong-Il contacted the KBS network and they connected him with Roy, who invited Dong-Il to watch the documentary with us.

At 5 p.m., I rush to the hotel lobby and immediately spot him; not because we look alike, but because I recognize the longing and anticipation in the way he stands there, unsure. Hand in pocket, hand out of pocket, smooth down the tie.

"I am Dong-Il," he nods and smiles warmly. I can't help myself. I reach out and embrace him.

Dong-Il lowers his head and hands me a gift—a black Mont Blanc pen with the words *Missing You* engraved along the side.

"Even if we are not brother and sister," he says gently, "someone is missing you all these years."

I look at him, unable to speak but wanting to say: Yes, something has been missing. I thank Dong-Il and we, along with Roy, Won, Seung-Hee, and Lee, squeeze into my hotel room to watch the documentary. Luckily, one wall of large floor-to-ceiling windows offers some sense of relief, because we can look out to the river and the city when scrutinizing one another's faces for something familiar becomes too much.

Over room service beers and champagne, Dong-Il explains that if I am the little sister, the "lost one" as she is called in the family, then I was not abandoned by his mother and father. I was possibly abducted and then abandoned or lost by the abductors. His mother has been searching for the lost daughter for 35 years and took a DNA test five years ago, thinking she might have found the Lost One. No matter what may come of this meeting, what happened to them is heartbreaking and reminds me, once again, that my story of loss and abandonment is not unique.

Dong-Il is tall and handsome, with an eagerness to please that is both charming and unsettling, revealing a sense of longing to be connected that is so familiar to me.

After watching the documentary, Dong-Il's sister calls and says: "I watched, too. She sounds like us. Don't force her, but ask if she will take a DNA test."

Roy's documentary airs to an audience of about 6 million. While it brilliantly captures my love for food and travel and the beginnings of my search for a birth family, there is no record of all that happened as a result, including the phone calls from families claiming me as theirs, and how I keep extending my stay in Seoul as new clues hint at why I was left behind. During press conferences for my book, I am told again how there were so many children abducted in the early 1970s; that it's very possible that I was really lost or kidnapped and not abandoned. Later I will think about this often and wonder how I might have to reshape my life minus the abandonment issues.

After my very last book interview, Roy calls to say that he has set up a DNA test for me. Dong-Il drives Won, who is kind enough to act as interpreter again, and me, negotiating the Friday afternoon streets of the city at top speed to Seoul University Hospital. I sign papers, and the rest is a blur. While Dong-Il and I make small talk about his job, there is some commotion about how

Dong-Il's mother left her DNA at the hospital five years prior when searching for the Lost Daughter and so only I need to give blood.

As the vice president in charge of the transportation division of his company, Dong-Il visits port cities around the world. We discover that we were both recently in New Orleans and stayed at the same hotel on the same day. We could have easily crossed paths as strangers in the lobby, the bar, or the elevator; now I'm waiting to see if he's my brother.

After, back at the hotel, with Lee in the lobby bar, Dong-Il explains that he and his family "discussed the possibility of you not being Lost One, because," he explains solemnly, then smiles, "no one is good cook in family." He laughs and says that, luckily, he married a woman who can cook. I appreciate his attempt at levity.

We order fresh fruit juice and beer, and as evening encroaches, we move on to $30 glasses of Veuve Clicquot. We toast to the story of life; to the possibility of similar bloodlines and markers; to the hope that our temporary family will become something more permanent.

I study Dong-Il as he glances every so often out over the city and takes a deep breath. When he catches me watching him, he smiles quickly and stares at me with sincere tenderness. I want to recognize myself in the shape of his eyes; lodge momentarily in the sparseness of his brow, the dark sheen of his hair; and mimic the deep, rich tones of his voice. We are, for the moment, connected.

"Maybe you are home," he tells me, reading my thoughts. He looks at the crease in my left elbow, where the cotton pokes out of the blood-crusted bandage. "Sister, I don't want you to be sad if we are not blood. I want to be your brother. I am your brother, no matter what blood says. We can choose home. We can choose family."

Soon it will be my last evening in Seoul, a rainy Sunday; Roy and my friends and I will meet for a farewell meal at a barbecue joint near Itaewon. Dong-Il will drive from his in-laws' house an hour south, wondering, hoping as I am, if this might be the beginning of many meals together. My editor and the foreign rights manager from Minumsa, my Korean publisher, both come and offer gifts of homemade plum syrup, a silk Korean apron, and beautiful handmade notebooks. Roy's wife and children are there, and so are Won, Seung-Hee, and Lee. We sit around the hot domed grill, steam rising between us as we devour juicy pork belly wrapped in sesame leaves, bowls of cold buckwheat noodles, and kimchi fried rice. We toast one another with *soju* and drink until our eyes shine bright and our hearts fill with the notion that we are somehow a family. Later, after I've returned to the United States, Roy will call, a rare sadness in his voice, to tell me that the blood test was deemed "inconclusive" and that I will have to return to continue the search.

For now, we are a temporary family. A gathering of people so different, and yet so similar in our hunger to be, at this moment, united. With each bite, I am as Korean as Roy, and as American as Lee; from as far west as California; and as present as this salt air, thick and full with the taste of home.

사 泗
사チヨン
천 川
대중식사

식	사	사기전		6,000
불	고	기쌈음		20,000
모	듬	전쌈		20,000
보		쌈음부		25,000
낙	지	음부장		20,000
사	천	부두		15,000
게		장		30,000

One of my most memorable days during the filming of Roy's documentary was spent with Seung-Hee, an interpreter who works for the Seoul government and who will soon be heading west to finish her PhD in human nutrition at Johns Hopkins. She and Roy confer and debate over where and what I should eat, tag-teaming to make sure I am getting my fair taste of Korean food; as if through tasting certain flavors, I could possibly remember faces, people, and a home.

Seung-Hee and I take a day to graze our way through the city. We start in my favorite neighborhood, Sam Saedong. I love the low and ancient houses filled with young designer ateliers, street food, family-style soup joints, and restaurants serving Royal Korean cuisine. We happily wait in line for flying pasta soup and Korean pancakes flecked with green onion and oyster. The weather is warm this early May, so we also try crushed ice mixed with tapioca and fresh fruit, which reminds me of sweet summertime New Orleans sno-balls, and I feel momentarily homesick. I suddenly long for Sundays with my family, when my grandfather would prepare a pot of crawfish bisque or gravy-smothered pork chops stuffed with oyster dressing.

During this visit, I'm discovering many similarities between Korean dishes and those of the American South, Louisiana in particular. Sundae, a Korean sausage made and eaten the same way as Cajun boudin, is often added to a soup with rice, which is very similar to Louisiana gumbo. Su-jae-bee is Korean-style chicken and dumplings (made with fish stock). And the Two-Two Fried Chicken chain (whose name always makes me smile) is not unlike our Southern Southern-fried bird, except with an extra super thin and crisp crust.

After a bowl of chicken stuffed with sticky rice, Seung-Hee leads me to a pot of boiled silkworms, and sausages on a stick wrapped in seaweed. People stop to tell me they saw me on the KBS documentary and in the newspapers and want to know if anyone has claimed me as theirs. Did I take a DNA test? I don't know what else to do but smile and defer to Seung-Hee.

"We have important things to do." Seung-Hee, sensing my longing for impossible answers, changes the subject. "We are lucky to be here this time of year. It's fresh preserved crab season. A true labor of love." And she's right. The freshest raw blue crabs are preserved in soy sauce, and after three days, you suck out beautiful translucent lump crabmeat jelly from the still-firm shell. After one bite, I know I want this sea taste forever.

"Sometimes," Seung-Hee warns with a smile, "they say, if you don't know how to make it right, the bacteria can cause temporary neurological damage; make you forget things."

We dig in for one more gorgeous ooze of crab knowing we are both thinking the same thing: Anything this good is worth a temporary lapse in memory.

bottoms-up rice

SERVES 4 TO 6

WHEN I WAS FIRST ADOPTED, I would often forgo cookies and milk and ask instead for a snack of steamed rice with just a pat of butter. And ever since I could stand by my grandfather's side and watch him cook, I've experimented with rice in all its forms. This is one of my favorite ways to offer the grain, both for flavor and presentation.

Some of the best dishes are the result of a beautiful blunder: Enter the French Tatin sisters and their famous upside-down apple tart. Once, I got distracted and forgot about a pot of rice on the stove and was pleasantly surprised to discover that with some modification, the mistake would soon become an oft-requested dish. This rice is delicious thanks to the golden crust that forms when cooking the grains a second time. This "golden bottom" goes by other names, including *tadig*, *concolón*, *soccarat*, and *nurungji* in Korean. I like shallots for the crust, but any thinly sliced white or yellow onion would also be good; it's best not to enlist scallions for this adventure. Some Persian friends use thinly sliced potato, lettuce leaves, or even very slim slices of bread to create the lovely buried treasure. Layer the bottom as nicely as possible, since it will be the top of the dish once it's turned out. The technique may seem difficult at first, but once you've made this rice several times, you'll become addicted.

For color and flavor, toss in a few saffron threads that have soaked in warm water. I make this in a heavy-bottomed nonstick 10-inch skillet to make turning out the rice easier.

bottoms-up rice

CONTINUED

1¼ cups long-grain rice (preferably basmati or jasmine)

½ teaspoon fine sea salt

1 tablespoon extra-virgin olive oil

1 tablespoon unsalted butter

¾ cup halved and thinly sliced shallots or yellow onion

Flaky finishing salt, for serving

1 Rinse the rice under running water several times, until the water is clear; drain.

2 Add the rinsed rice, 2¼ cups water, and the salt to a 10-inch nonstick skillet and bring to a boil. Decrease the heat to low and simmer, covered, for 14 minutes. Turn off the heat and let sit, covered, for 5 minutes. Empty the rice into a large bowl, draining any excess water. Wipe out the bottom of the pan with a paper towel. Heat the oil and butter in the skillet over medium-high heat until frothy. Add the shallots, stirring occasionally, and let cook for about 3 minutes. Spread the shallots in a single layer across the bottom of the skillet. Gently and evenly spread the rice over the shallots, smoothing the top with a rubber spatula or large spoon. Cover the pan with a tight-fitting lid and cook on medium-high heat for 2 minutes. You want the heat high enough to crisp and toast the rice and shallot layer without burning it. Decrease the heat to the lowest setting and let steam, covered, for another 5 minutes. Turn off the heat and let the rice sit, covered, for another 5 minutes or so, until ready to serve.

3 To serve, carefully and swiftly turn the rice over onto a serving platter, like an upside-down cake, so that the golden side is bottoms up. Serve at once with a sprinkle of flaky finishing salt.

quick pickled fennel

MAKES ABOUT 4 CUPS

SLIGHTLY SWEET AND AROMATIC fennel is a refreshing contrast to sticky, sweet, and spicy Korean barbecue. I like to serve this with the traditional *banchan* or Korean side dishes, and on sandwiches in place of pickles. Adding a pinch or two of coarse Korean red chile powder (*gochugaru*) or ground cayenne adds color and a bit of heat.

1 small fennel bulb (about 15 ounces), trimmed and very thinly sliced; some fronds reserved

4 to 6 fresh Thai green chiles

1 cup apple cider vinegar

½ cup water

2 tablespoons sugar

2 teaspoons pickling salt or fine sea salt

¼ teaspoon gochugaru (coarse Korean red chile powder) or cayenne pepper (optional)

1 Place the sliced fennel, some of the fronds, and the Thai chiles in a widemouth 1-quart jar, leaving 1 inch of room at the top of the jar. Place the vinegar, water, sugar, and salt in a medium pot over medium-high heat, whisking to combine. Bring to a simmer, stirring until the sugar dissolves. Pour the mixture over the fennel and chiles, making sure to cover completely with liquid but still leaving 1 inch of space at the top of the jar. Let cool to room temperature. Add the *gochugaru*. Cover with a tight-fitting lid; turn the jar upside down a few times and refrigerate for at least a day or two before eating. The pickled fennel will keep stored in the refrigerator for up to 2 weeks.

pork belly korean-style bbq

SERVES 6 TO 8

I'LL ALWAYS REMEMBER that farewell meal of Korean barbecue with my makeshift Korean family back in 2008. Seeking out a good rendition, I spoke with Chef Heong Soon Park, who shared his recipe that he serves at Seattle's Chan Restaurant, an intimate space with an open kitchen where Park cooks the way Korean food is heading—healthier, smaller portions with local touches, including bulgogi sliders with microgreens and smoked chile mayo, and spicy golden rice cakes with house-made kimchi and mustard seed. At Chan, Park makes the basic sauce for the pork and varies it by adding puréed kimchi or onion to mellow out the sweetness. This marinade is also good with thinly sliced pork butt, which Park prefers because it has enough fat but not as much as the belly. He also uses the marinade to baste pork ribs or lamb chops. Of the marinade, he notes, "This is a basic sauce, which will be very sweet, but once you add pork, it will mellow out; also, the flavor is supposed to be sweet at first and with a hint of spice at the end."

Koreans use a heated grill plate placed in the center of the table so that everyone can cook at their leisure. This is convivial but not always practical for the home cook, so that's why I've adapted this for the outdoor grill as well as for a standard home oven. You can find the *gochujang* and *gochugaru* at most Asian markets or online.

pork belly korean-style bbq

1 (¼-inch-thick, 3-pound) slab pork belly

¼ cup gochujang (Korean fermented soybean-chile paste)

1 tablespoon gochugaru (coarse Korean red chile powder)

⅓ cup soy sauce

3 tablespoons light brown sugar

2 tablespoons honey

2 tablespoons sesame oil

2 tablespoons mirin

1 tablespoon unseasoned rice vinegar

4 to 6 large cloves garlic, minced

For serving: lettuce leaves, green perilla (sesame) leaves, cooked rice, and a variety of Korean side dishes, such as kimchi, firm tofu poached in sesame oil topped with toasted sesame seeds and thinly sliced green onion

1 Slice the pork into ½-inch-thick slices and layer in a shallow dish. Make the marinade by combining the *gochujang*, *gochugaru*, soy sauce, brown sugar, honey, sesame oil, mirin, rice vinegar, and garlic in a medium saucepan over medium heat; stir and cook until the sugar dissolves. Turn off the heat and let cool to room temperature.

2 Pour half of the marinade over the pork, cover, and let marinate in the refrigerator for at least 2 hours and up to 6 hours.

3 Heat a grill to 425° to 450°F. Remove the pork belly from the refrigerator, and drain and discard the marinade. Grill the pork belly slices for about 3 minutes per side, or until crispy, caramelized, and cooked through; watch the grill carefully for flare-ups due to the pork belly fat. Cut the pork, using scissors, into bite-size pieces. Serve with the accompaniments of choice.

NOTE: If you prefer, roast the pork belly slices, uncovered, in a preheated 450°F oven for about 30 minutes, turning once and basting with more marinade, or until crispy and caramelized.

pork shoulder korean-style bbq

Substitute 1 (3- to 4-pound) pork butt, trimmed of excess fat, for the pork belly. Pour three-quarters of the marinade over; cover and refrigerate for 1 hour. Preheat the oven to 350°F. Place the marinated pork butt in a large pan, cover tightly with a lid or aluminum foil, and bake for 1 hour. Baste the pork with the remaining marinade and let cook for another 2 hours, adding a bit of water or orange juice if it begins to stick to the bottom of the pan, or until the pork is fork-tender. Pull the meat apart with forks or slice and serve with the accompaniments of choice.

basic fresh kimchi

MAKES ABOUT 6 CUPS

MENTION KIMCHI and watch many people squinch up their nose. Admittedly, it has a bit of a stinky reputation, but I love it just when it's about to turn funky yet still maintains its crunch and vigor. For the kimchi averse, I make this quick recipe that is more like a salad and does not require fermentation, as traditional kimchi does. I like to make this with napa cabbage, bok choy, or green cabbage. Many recipes call for a sweet rice paste to help bind the spices to the cabbage, but you can also use pear juice. For more delicate palates, decrease the amount of chile powder.

Serve with Pork Belly Korean-Style BBQ (page 14), as a side salad to grilled meats and fish, on tacos or sandwiches, puréed into soups, or over steamed rice.

1 medium to large head napa cabbage (about 2 pounds), trimmed of any loose or discolored leaves

2 tablespoons salt

1 firm but ripe pear (preferably Asian), cored and chopped

¾ cup gochugaru (coarse Korean red chile powder; for a less spicy version decrease to ½ cup)

¼ cup coarsely grated fresh ginger

2 tablespoons light soy sauce

1 to 2 tablespoons ground chile paste, such as sambal oelek

1 tablespoon fish sauce (optional)

4 to 6 cloves garlic

4 carrots (about 6 ounces), cut into 2-inch matchsticks

1 medium daikon radish, cut into 2-inch matchsticks

1 Cut the cabbage lengthwise into quarters; remove the core, and chop into about 1-inch-wide (bite-size) pieces. Place half of the cabbage in a large colander in the sink; sprinkle with 1 tablespoon of the salt. Add the remaining half of the cabbage and top with the remaining 1 tablespoon salt. Let sit for 10 minutes. Using tongs or your hands, turn the cabbage so that the bottom layer is on top; let sit for another 15 minutes. Rinse the cabbage, drain thoroughly, and pat dry or spin dry in a salad spinner.

2 Combine the pear, *gochugaru*, ginger, soy sauce, chile paste, fish sauce, if using, and garlic in the bowl of a food processor and pulse until just blended. Pour the mixture into a large bowl. Add the carrots and radish; toss to combine. Add the drained cabbage; toss to combine. Let sit, covered, in the refrigerator for 30 minutes. Drain again. Store in an airtight container in the refrigerator for 3 to 4 days. It's still good for up to a week or so, but it will start getting a little funky and taste more like the fermented kimchi of ill repute.

samgaetong
(ginseng chicken soup)

SERVES 2 TO 4

ALMOST EVERY CULTURE has a version of chicken in a pot—arroz con pollo, chicken matzoh ball soup, poule au pot—and the Koreans have *samgaetong*, ginseng chicken soup. I've been told by some Korean culinary traditionalists that they don't salt their broth, as it changes the texture of the meat. Instead, they sometimes offer a bowl of dipping salt and pepper at the table. I like adding salt to the different layers in this dish, but you could omit it in the cooking process and serve it on the side. At the risk of some Korean granny finger wagging, after about 40 minutes, I like to add one quartered onion and a couple of sliced carrots to the broth. Let cook for another 20 minutes, or until the chicken is tender and falling off the bone. You can find most of these ingredients in Asian markets. Some even have a *samgaetong* package with jujube, ginseng, and dried chestnut included.

¾ cup sticky rice

2¾ teaspoons sea salt

¾ teaspoon freshly
ground black pepper

6 cloves garlic, peeled

1 (2-inch piece) Korean ginseng
or fresh ginger, minced

10 dried jujubes (Chinese dates)
or dried California dates

5 to 6 gingko nuts or
¼ cup pine nuts

1 (2- to 3-pound) chicken
or 2 Cornish hens

Fresh chestnuts (optional)

1 medium yellow
onion, quartered

2 carrots, sliced into coins

Sesame oil and sliced
green onion, for garnish

1 Soak the rice, covered in cold water, overnight. Drain the rice and combine in a bowl with ¼ teaspoon of the salt, ¼ teaspoon of the pepper, 2 to 3 of the garlic cloves, half of the minced ginger, 3 to 4 jujubes, and 3 to 4 gingko nuts; set aside.

2 Rinse the chicken with hot water. Lightly season the inside of the cavity with ½ teaspoon of the salt (a bit less if using Cornish hens). Stuff the rice mixture deep into the cavity of the chicken. You can close it up with a toothpick, if desired, but it's not necessary, as the rice will stick together as it cooks.

3 Place the chicken in a large pot and cover with water. Bring to a boil and skim the froth after about 10 minutes. Stir in the remaining 2 teaspoons salt and the remaining ½ teaspoon pepper. Add the remaining garlic cloves, minced ginger, jujubes, and gingko nuts. Add the chestnuts, if using, to the broth. Decrease the heat to medium-low and simmer for about 45 minutes. (If adding onion and carrots, add to the broth after 20 minutes.) Taste and add more salt and pepper as needed. The rice should be sticky and translucent. Remove the chicken from the pot. Spoon the rice out of the chicken cavity into serving bowls. Remove the meat from the bones and pour the broth and chicken over the rice. Drizzle each bowl with a bit of sesame oil and top with sliced green onion.

"back to heaven" quince tea

MAKES 4 CUPS

ONE AFTERNOON, poet Lee Herrick and I slipped into a small bookshop and tearoom in the Insadong neighborhood of Seoul named after the poetry collection *Back to Heaven* by Korean poet Ch'on Sang Pyong. Later, Seung-Hee and I returned for another taste of paradise.

Every time I remember this tea, it takes me back to a time and place of peace—one of the few moments during those weeks in Seoul when I wasn't sleepless and stressed about possibly finding my birth family. This tea is delicious chilled or warm; you just have to plan ahead to prepare the quince at least 2 weeks in advance. In place of quince, try kumquat, or yuzu citrus peel with fresh ginger.

1 pound quince (about 2), peeled, cored, quartered, and thinly sliced crosswise

2 cups sugar

1 In a sterilized widemouthed 1-quart jar, evenly layer some of the quince slices, some of the sugar, and more quince slices; repeat, ending with a layer of sugar. Seal the jar and let sit on the kitchen counter for at least 2 weeks and up to 1 month, turning upside down occasionally to evenly distribute the sugar and juices that will form.

2 For 1 cup of tea, put 2 tablespoons of the preserved quince in a mug and pour boiling water over. Serve hot or chilled.

I. if i am what i eat

Then I am the raw jellied crab
oozing on the tongue as we sit
in a small, hot room in Insadong
where you, a man I have known my whole life,
have come to take pause in this search of a birth mother.

This is all we have
this crab, only this time of year, in this part of the world.
Years ago, they warned eating it this way could cause
temporary memory loss.

But that smile on your face
as you slurp the sea from one of the legs
and the heat of you, broad golden moon, eyes
dark like hot stones.
No one will ever know if those are tears
or small birds in flight,
like the moments of our childhood
no one recorded
as if remembering would be too much.
This temporary moment of forgetting
is all we have and somehow, worth it all.

II. if you are what you eat

Then you are the salted tomatoes and capers
from climbing twisted vines in a town dusted with departure
and feverish kisses to the cheek, the neck, the underside of the palm

as a small boat awaits you.
Let us share one last bowl of pasta, you suggest,
with anchovy, hot pepper, a swipe of thick
country bread drenched in bittersweet golden oil.

III. if i am what you eat

I am the mother lode
the 200-year-old Istrian yeast for a biga
so sweet and swollen,
a handful of golden raisins, saffron threads from a song
I used to know by heart.
A song I sing
Because I am what you are.

IV. if you are what i eat

Then you will be a hot, puffed doughnut
filled with vanilla-flecked cream.
I will be the moon rising
and dusting the orchards with light and air
water and wind.
Because if you are what I eat
then I will no longer eat fear

the way I used to
when I thought danger
could slip into a bowl of noodles
like an unseen poison
like the hatred in countries
in the blackened hearts
of people who know nothing of themselves.

Because you are what I am
then I will be love
and the memories of your childhood
and this
is worth everything.

sticky rice with persimmon *and* sesame

SERVES 4 TO 6

RICE FOR DESSERT? Many Asian cultures incorporate the grain into a sweet treat, especially using sticky rice, the nutty, glutinous variety that I love to eat with Thai curries and other saucy dishes, as it elevates the texture and flavor of the curry, and also acts as a nice palate cushion for the hotter versions that I tend to prefer. As dessert, sticky rice is sweetened with coconut milk and sugar, then most commonly topped with sliced fresh mango. Depending on the season, try substituting fresh ripe fig, peach, papaya, or kiwi.

1½ cups sticky rice (also called glutinous or sweet rice)

1 (13½-ounce) can thick coconut milk, stirred

½ cup lightly packed brown sugar

½ teaspoon salt

2 ripe Hachiya persimmons, mangos, peaches, or papayas, or 3 kiwi

Toasted sesame seeds, fresh Thai basil, and fresh cilantro, for garnish

1 Soak the rice, covered in cold water, overnight. Drain the rice well in a fine-mesh sieve. Steam the rice, covered, in the top part of a steamer lined with cheesecloth (be careful to not let the steamer basket touch the water) for about 30 minutes, or until the rice is tender and glossy. You can also steam the rice in a traditional conical rice steamer, covered with a lid.

2 While the rice is steaming, pour the coconut milk into a heavy-bottomed pan over medium-high heat. Add the sugar and salt and stir. Do not let the milk boil, but do heat and stir until the sugar dissolves.

3 When the rice is cooked, pour it into a large bowl. Pour 1 cup of the warm milk mixture over the rice, and stir gently to combine; let sit for at least 10 minutes to allow the rice to soak up the flavors. Place a mound of sticky rice on each serving plate, top with sliced fruit, and drizzle with the remaining milk mixture. Garnish with sesame seeds and herbs.

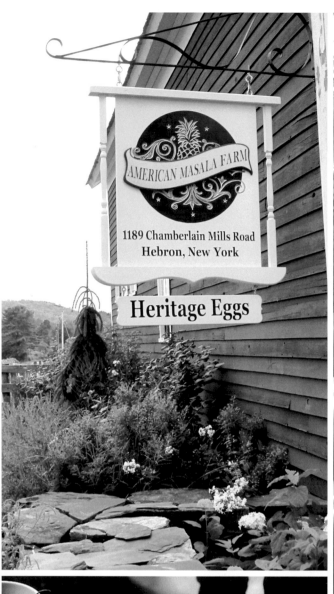

AMERICAN MASALA FARM

1189 Chamberlain Mills Road
Hebron, New York

Heritage Eggs

girl on fire

I'VE ALWAYS FAVORED SAVORY OVER SWEET and hot over mild, even as a young child. I was about four years old when I first tasted "Mexican" food. My parents had taken my younger sister and me to a Tex-Mex restaurant in San Antonio. My sister used to call it "the Mexi-can in San An-Tokyo." We were two Asian girls fresh from orphanages in Korea and what did we know? We were visiting from New Orleans and hungry for anything that resembled food and love. Later, my sister and I, looking to amuse ourselves, would open jars of store-bought hot salsa and pickled jalapeños. On the count of three, we would dig in with tortilla chips and continue to eat until one of us would give up, mouth on fire, running to the kitchen for bread or water. As my taste for Mexican and other "hot" cuisines, such as North African and Indian, has evolved, I've never lost my love for heat, the resulting tears that well up, and that addictive feverish tingle from a good hot pepper burn. To cool things down, as well as dairy-rich condiments and breads, I like to include refreshing salads, like Kachoombar Salad (page 40) and Carrot with Orange Blossom Salad (page 34), in the mix.

Carrot with Orange
Blossom Salad, page 34

vegetable couscous with lamb sausage

SERVES 6 TO 8

BEFORE I EVER TRAVELED TO NORTH AFRICA, I had friends in Paris and Provence of North African descent; in France, Algerians and Moroccans make up a large portion of the Arab population. This recipe is a combination of couscous and tagine recipes often cooked by two different women I knew, and who were both highly competitive when it came to their national cuisine. Yasmina, of Algerian descent, preferred mutton with her couscous, while Zorah, from Morocco, favored lots of vegetables and briny additions like olives and preserved lemon.

For a vegetarian feast, omit the lamb sausage in this recipe, use vegetable broth in place of the chicken stock, and add green olives or preserved lemons.

vegetable couscous with lamb sausage

1 tablespoon olive oil

4 links lamb sausage (preferably merguez; about 1 pound), halved

1 large yellow onion, halved and sliced into ¼-inch pieces

2 cloves garlic, minced

1½ teaspoons sea salt

1 teaspoon ground cinnamon

1 tablespoon grated fresh ginger

3 pounds mixed seasonal vegetables, such as: 1 small pumpkin (about 12 ounces), peeled, seeded, and diced; carrots, halved lengthwise and cut into thirds; turnips, cut into 2-inch pieces; zucchini, halved lengthwise and cut into thirds

1 cup golden raisins

5 cups chicken stock or vegetable broth

1 (15½-ounce) can chickpeas

1 (10-ounce) package plain couscous

1 tablespoon unsalted butter

1 cup boiling water

Toasted almonds or pistachios, for garnish

Fresh cilantro or mint leaves, for garnish

Harissa, for serving

1 Heat the oil in a large heavy-bottom pot over medium heat. Add the sausage and cook for about 5 minutes. Add the onion and sauté for 3 minutes; add the garlic and sauté for another minute. Add ¾ teaspoon of the salt, the cinnamon, ginger, vegetables (except the zucchini, if using), and raisins; stir well. Add the stock and bring to a boil. Decrease the heat and simmer for 20 minutes, until the pumpkin is tender when pierced with a fork. Stir in the zucchini (if using) and chickpeas; simmer for about 10 minutes, until the zucchini is tender but not mushy.

2 Pour the couscous into a large bowl with the remaining ¾ teaspoon of salt and the butter. Add the boiling water and stir to combine. Cover tightly with plastic wrap and let sit for 5 minutes. Steam the couscous for 5 minutes using a couscoussier or in the top of a steamer basket lined with cheesecloth or a clean kitchen towel. Pour the couscous into a large bowl and gently roll the grains between your hands to separate them. Then pour back into the steamer basket and keep warm until ready to serve.

3 To serve, pile the couscous in the center of a large platter. Remove the sausage and vegetables from the pot and arrange around the couscous. Garnish with almonds and cilantro. Pour the broth from the pot into a ladle and stir in about 1 teaspoon of harissa and then pour over the couscous and vegetables.

harissa, mon amour

MAKES 2 CUPS

WHEN I VISITED TUNISIA YEARS AGO, I lost one love (a maddening and unfaithful poet) but left with many new ones—all culinary, and much more reliable. Among these were fragrant orange blossom cookies, a technique for hot buttered hand-rolled couscous, the scent of warm moons of semolina bread, and my favorite: tubes of a spicy condiment called harissa, which I stashed in my suitcase. The prepared paste was thick and hot, with a bit of smokiness. I've since experimented with several homemade versions, and I like this one the best. Sometimes I add fresh mint as well as dried, and a squeeze of fresh orange juice. If you like a milder flavor, add more tomato paste or a small cooked carrot to the mix.

There are so many wonderful ways to taste harissa: spread on warm flatbread; tossed with grilled vegetables; rubbed under chicken skin and grilled; and stirred into soups or the broth of tagines—North African stews—and served with steamed couscous.

1 teaspoon caraway seeds

1 teaspoon coriander seeds

1 teaspoon cumin seeds

1½ cups chopped red Fresno chiles (about 12 chiles; they look like red jalapeños)

1½ teaspoons fine sea salt

Pinch of dried mint (optional)

5 to 6 cloves garlic, peeled

2 tablespoons freshly squeezed lemon juice

1 tablespoon thick tomato paste

1 whole (about ⅓ cup) jarred roasted red bell pepper, drained (about ⅓ cup)

Extra-virgin olive oil, for topping

1. Heat the caraway, coriander, and cumin seeds in a small skillet over medium heat, and toast the spices, swirling the skillet, until fragrant and just starting to turn color. Be careful not to burn them; but if you do, just start over. Grind the toasted spices in a spice grinder or with a mortar and pestle.

2. Place the toasted and ground spices, chiles, salt, mint, garlic, lemon juice, and tomato paste in the skillet; cook, stirring occasionally, over low heat, about 5 minutes. Transfer to a blender or food processor and pulse until smooth, stopping occasionally to scrape down the sides. Add the roasted red bell pepper and blend until smooth. Transfer the pepper paste to a container (a sterilized glass jar is best). Top with a thin layer of olive oil. Cover and refrigerate, topping off with more oil after each use. Store in the refrigerator for up to 2 weeks.

carrot *with* orange blossom salad

SERVES 4 TO 6

VERSIONS OF THIS BEAUTIFUL SALAD are served throughout the Middle East, especially in Morocco and Tunisia. It's fragrant with a touch of orange flower water, which can be found in the baking section of your local market or in specialty markets. Serve between the main course and dessert or as part of a larger feast, especially as it helps balance out the more spice-laden dishes.

2 tablespoons confectioners' sugar

¼ teaspoon fine sea salt

1 teaspoon orange flower water

Juice of 1 lemon

8 medium carrots, peeled and grated (about 3 cups)

2 oranges, peeled, white pith removed, and sliced into ⅛-inch rounds or half-moons

1 tablespoon extra-virgin olive oil

Fresh mint leaves, for garnish

½ teaspoon ground cinnamon

1 Whisk together 1 tablespoon of the sugar, the salt, orange flower water, and lemon juice in a medium bowl. Add the carrots and toss to combine. The salad can be made ahead at this point and refrigerated for up to 2 days.

2 Remove the carrots from the refrigerator 30 minutes before serving and place on a serving platter. Top with the orange slices, drizzle the olive oil over, and top with mint leaves. At the table or just before serving, combine the remaining 1 tablespoon sugar and the cinnamon in a fine-mesh sieve and tap the side of the sieve to sprinkle evenly over the salad.

pan-fried peppers with coconut and tamarind

SERVES 6 TO 8

THIS IS ONE OF MY FAVORITE Indian dishes inspired by my good friend, chef Suvir Saran. When he was working on his book, *Masala Farm*, his partner, Charlie, and I happily volunteered to test this recipe for him; we both make it with hotter chiles and eat it until tears run down our cheeks and are both gasping for air. I have since modified it ever so slightly; Suvir calls for peanut flour, but I like to sometimes use Bob's Red Mill almond or coconut flour. Suvir's clever use of both sweet and hot peppers makes for a beautiful balance of flavors. Serve warm with rice, raita, and Kachoombar Salad (page 40).

we both make it with hotter chiles and eat it until tears run down our cheeks

pan-fried peppers ~with~ coconut and tamarind

SPICE MIX
MAKES 1 CUP

3 tablespoons black mustard seeds

2 tablespoons cumin seeds

2 tablespoons coriander seeds

2 tablespoons white sesame seeds

1 teaspoon whole cloves

1 teaspoon green cardamom seeds

1 tablespoon black peppercorns

6 small dried red chile peppers

PEPPERS

⅓ cup plus 2 tablespoons canola oil

1 pound hot fresh chiles, such as habanero, jalapeño, and serrano, seeded and cut into 1-inch pieces

1½ pounds mixed red, orange, and yellow bell peppers, cut into 1-inch pieces

1½ pounds milder fresh chiles, like poblano and Anaheim, seeded and cut into 1-inch pieces

½ cup almond or coconut flour, such as Bob's Red Mill

1 cup unsweetened shredded coconut

2 teaspoons salt

2 tablespoons tamarind paste (not concentrate), softened in a bit of warm water

1   To make the spice mix, combine all of the spices and dried chiles in a spice grinder or coffee grinder and grind to a coarse powder. Reserve 1 cup and store the rest in an airtight container, preferably in the refrigerator, for up to several months.

2   To make the peppers, heat 2 tablespoons of the oil in a large pan, like a wok, over high heat. Sauté all of the chiles and bell peppers, stirring occasionally, until lightly blistered, 18 to 20 minutes. Remove the chiles and peppers from the pan and reserve.

3   Add the remaining ⅓ cup oil to the pan along with the reserved spice mix. Decrease the heat to medium-high and fry the spice mix, stirring constantly, for 2 minutes. Add the almond flour and stir, scraping the bottom and sides of the pan. Deglaze the pan with 1 cup water, scraping the bottom of the pan to remove any cooked-on bits. Cook, stirring constantly, for 2 minutes more (be careful not to burn the flour). If the heat is too high, decrease it to medium. Add another cup of water and stir to combine the water and spice mix; cook for 3 minutes more, until a bit of oil begins to form on the top. Add the shredded coconut and stir; cook for 4 to 5 minutes. Add the salt and tamarind paste and stir to combine, about 1 minute. Add 2 cups of water and stir to combine. Add the reserved chiles and peppers. Cover and cook on medium-high heat for about 7 minutes, adding up to 1 cup more water depending on how much sauce you like. Taste and add more salt as needed. The pan-fried peppers can be made 1 day ahead and reheated before serving.

curry leaf cocktail

SERVES 1

I COOK A LOT WITH curry leaves, especially after having spent summers cooking with Indian chef Suvir Saran and his partner, Charlie Burd, at their American Masala Farm in upstate New York. And as I have experimented over the years with ways to infuse simple syrups, I've found that curry leaf makes for a super-fragrant and spiced hit of syrup. I like it with a dry sparkling wine or mixed with gin, muddled cucumber, lime juice, and mint.

CURRY LEAF
SIMPLE SYRUP

1 cup water

1 cup sugar

A few drops of freshly squeezed lemon juice

About 20 fresh curry leaves

Brut Champagne or sparkling wine, such as prosecco or cava

Cucumber spear, for garnish

1 To make the simple syrup, combine the water and sugar in a small pot. Bring to a low boil, stirring occasionally. Add a few drops of lemon juice to keep the sugar from crystallizing. Add the curry leaves. Remove from the heat and let steep for about 1 hour. Remove the curry leaves and chill until ready to use. The syrup will keep for up to 2 weeks.

2 For each cocktail, pour 1 to 2 teaspoons simple syrup into each champagne flute; fill the rest of the way with Champagne. Garnish with the spear of cucumber.

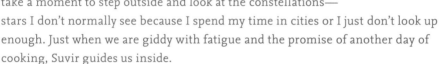

kachoombar salad

SERVES 4

EVERYONE I'VE EVER MADE THIS FOR falls for the
fresh combination of ingredients. It's a super-simple salad and
a wonderful accompaniment to spicier dishes. This is another
recipe inspired by Suvir Saran. When I'm lucky, sometimes
I am able to spend part of the summer with Suvir and his
partner, Charlie, on their farm in upstate New York. We
indulge in cooking together from sunrise until Suvir makes us
take a moment to step outside and look at the constellations—
stars I don't normally see because I spend my time in cities or I just don't look up
enough. Just when we are giddy with fatigue and the promise of another day of
cooking, Suvir guides us inside.

"Kimlet, it's time to sleep," he tells me. "In the morning, I will bake you
biscuits and make jam and Charlie will have fresh coffee. Fat blueberries,
peaches, and tomatoes are waiting for us. . . ."

In this recipe, Suvir calls for tomatoes; but in the winter, I usually just use
cucumber and apple, and maybe a crisp Asian pear as well.

**1 English cucumber,
peeled and seeded**

**2 apples (1 tart and 1 sweet),
cored and chopped**

1 cup halved cherry tomatoes

Juice of ½ lime

**3 tablespoons mixed chopped
fresh mint and cilantro**

**½ teaspoon toasted and
ground cumin seeds (optional)**

**1 small fresh jalapeño, stemmed,
seeded, and diced (optional)**

Sea salt

1 Gently combine the cucumber, apples, and tomatoes in a
medium bowl. Stir in the lime juice, herbs, cumin seeds, if
using, and jalapeño, if using. If making ahead, chill until
ready to serve. Add a bit of sea salt to taste, just before
serving.

NOTE: Sometimes I add a drizzle of tangerine oil from
Pasolivo in Paso Robles, California. And if there is any salad
left over, I mix it with yogurt for an impromptu raita.

tacos anonymous

I HAVE HAD A LIFELONG LOVE AFFAIR with tacos. A taco
was a beautiful thing to behold and one of my favorite meals when I
was growing up. Admittedly, the Friday night treat of crunchy prefab
shells topped with ground meat, canned sliced olives, and shredded
orange cheese had its place amid the weeknight pots of jambalaya and
gumbo. My tastes have evolved—I love soft shells now, fresh corn
tortillas hot off the griddle. Tacos are best enjoyed with other taco
addicts, and I luckily know many of them.

roast pork tacos

SERVES 8 TO 10

SOME OF THE BEST FOOD IN MEXICO, including tacos, I've found is roadside, from street carts, and at small *loncherias* or lunch counters often found in local markets. I first tasted one of my favorites, *tacos al pastor,* just outside of San Miguel de Allende in central Mexico. Similar to schwarma, spit-cooked meat brought by the Lebanese to Mexico, *tacos al pastor* features pork marinated in chiles and cooked rotisserie-style.

One late night, photographer Rick Lew and I were on a tequila-and-taco mission after a long day of shooting a food story for *Cottage Living* magazine. Someone had directed us to just outside of the city to the "best *tacos al pastor.*" We were about to give up, exhausted and hungry, when there before us stood a tall vertical spit glinting with juicy layers of whole pork butts crowned with an entire fresh pineapple. We watched as the vendor cradled a freshly made hot corn tortilla in the palm of one hand and, swiftly with the other, sliced shavings of both meat and pineapple in one fell swoop onto the tortilla. A squeeze of lime and a sprinkling of chopped onion and cilantro and suddenly we weren't so tired anymore. We ate our very fair share and quite happily moved on to tequila tasting around town.

I don't go for very long without someone asking me to make a taco fiesta, and roast pork is often a favorite. For an easy home version, I roast the pork shoulder until fork-tender and serve it with a variety of garnishes, including grilled pineapple. You could also add chunks of fresh pineapple to the roasting pan during the last hour of cooking. I like to serve the meat in fresh hot corn tortillas or cabbage leaves.

roast pork tacos

CONTINUED

You might find pork butt labeled as picnic, pork shoulder, or Boston butt. Since there's a generous amount of fat and connective tissue, this is the perfect cut for low and slow cooking. I use boneless or bone-in, depending on what the butcher has available.

3 tablespoons light brown sugar

3 tablespoons fine sea salt

1 (6- to 7-pound) whole boneless pork butt or shoulder

2 ounces New Mexico red chile powder (usually in the Hispanic section; otherwise use a good-quality pure ground chile powder)

1 tablespoon dried oregano

6 cloves garlic, minced

1 teaspoon ground cumin

¼ teaspoon ground cinnamon

1 (12-ounce) bottle brown ale

1 large yellow onion, quartered

1 orange, quartered

½ fresh pineapple, cut into chunks (optional)

For serving: cabbage leaves, fresh corn tortillas, Roasted Tomatillo-Poblano Salsa (page 46), grilled pineapple chunks, thinly sliced cabbage, lime wedges, radish slices, sliced fresh jalapeños, sour cream, queso fresco, and/or fresh cilantro

1. Combine the sugar and salt in a small bowl. Place the pork in a roasting pan or Dutch oven and rub the sugar-salt mixture all over. Cover and let sit in the refrigerator for 4 hours or up to 24 hours.

2. Preheat the oven to 350°F.

3. Remove the pork from the pan and discard any excess liquid. Rinse the pork, pat dry, and place it back in the clean roasting pan.

4. Combine the red chile powder with the oregano, garlic, cumin, and cinnamon in a small bowl and mix to combine. Rub the spice mixture all over the pork. Pour the beer over the pork. Cover the pan tightly with the lid or aluminum foil and bake for 2 hours.

5. Uncover the pork and add the onion and 3 quarters of the orange (save 1 quarter for squeezing over the pork just before serving). Decrease the heat to 325°F and cook for another 1 to 2 hours. If using, add the pineapple chunks during the last hour of cooking. The pork should be tender and easily pulled with a fork; if the fork test does not work, cook for another 30 minutes and test again. Remove from the oven and let sit, covered or lightly tented with foil, for up to 30 minutes. Use forks to gently pull apart the meat. Squeeze the juice from the remaining orange quarter over the pork and serve with the accompaniments.

6. To make a taco, place the roasted pork in a cabbage leaf or tortilla, and top with salsa, radish slices, cilantro, and a squeeze of lime.

cilantro-jalapeño margarita

SERVES 1

ALTHOUGH MEXICAN IN ORIGIN, this particular recipe was inspired by the Haili'imaile General Store, a Bev Gannon restaurant, in the beautiful and vast upcountry of Maui. Freshly squeezed juice of orange, lemon, and lime is combined with a subtly spiced simple syrup. The jalapeño in the syrup offers a slow, sneaky heat.

CILANTRO-JALAPEÑO SIMPLE SYRUP

1 cup water

1 cup sugar

2 or 3 fresh jalapeños, split lengthwise

½ bunch fresh cilantro

A few drops of freshly squeezed lemon juice

Salt, for rimming

1½ ounces tequila (preferably blanco 100% agave)

1 ounce equal parts of freshly squeezed lime, orange, and lemon juices

Jalapeño slice, for garnish

Cilantro sprig, for garnish

1 To make the simple syrup, combine the water, sugar, jalapeños, and cilantro in a medium pot over medium-high heat and cook until it begins to simmer, stirring occasionally until the sugar dissolves, about 3 minutes. Add a few drops of lemon juice to prevent the sugar from crystallizing. Turn off the heat and let cool. Strain before using. Store in the refrigerator for up to 2 weeks.

2 For each cocktail, rim a margarita glass or lowball glass with salt. Add the tequila, freshly squeezed juices, and 1 to 2 teaspoons of the simple syrup to a cocktail shaker half-filled with ice and shake to combine. Strain into the rimmed glass, and garnish with a jalapeño slice and a cilantro sprig.

roasted tomatillo-poblano salsa

MAKES ABOUT 1½ CUPS

SALSAS COME IN ALL SORTS OF COLORS and flavors in Mexico, and it's fun to try different chiles and preparation methods, including raw, roasted, or grilled. I love my salsa hot, hot, hot, so I don't always remove the seeds from the chiles, but you can remove the ribs and seeds for a milder version. If you choose not to wear gloves when preparing the chiles, be careful not to touch your eyes or other sensitive areas before washing your hands thoroughly with soap and water. I roast these chiles, but you can also grill the vegetables for a smoky flavor; and once you've whizzed everything up, if the salsa is still too hot, add more avocado or even half a peeled cucumber. Serve with tortilla chips or as a garnish for tacos with pork, chicken, or fish.

6 to 8 tomatillos, husked and quartered

3 fresh poblano or Anaheim chiles, stemmed and quartered

2 to 3 fresh jalapeño or serrano chiles, stemmed, seeded if desired, and halved

1 large white or yellow onion, peeled and quartered

2 cloves garlic, peeled

1 teaspoon sea salt

½ cup fresh cilantro

½ teaspoon toasted ground cumin seeds (optional)

1 ripe avocado, pitted and peeled

Juice of 2 limes

1 Preheat the oven to 425°F.

2 Spread the tomatillos, chiles, onion, and garlic in a single layer on a baking sheet and season with the salt. Roast for 15 to 20 minutes, until tender and starting to blister. Let cool slightly.

3 Combine the roasted vegetables and any of the escaped juices with the cilantro in the bowl of a food processor, and pulse until well blended but not puréed. Add the cumin seeds, if using, the avocado, and lime juice and pulse until just blended. Taste and add more salt and lime, as needed. Store in an airtight container in the refrigerator for up to 3 days.

FOR A FRESH VERSION: Reduce the amount of poblano/Anaheim to 1 and omit roasting the vegetables; pulse everything in a food processor until well blended. Taste and add more avocado, lime juice, or salt.

tomato-habanero salsa

MAKES 1 CUP

THIS IS A QUICK NO-COOK
salsa recipe that I have had versions of
throughout Mexico and the Caribbean
islands. The natural sweetness of tomato
balances out the heat of the habanero chile
in this smooth, spicy sauce. Serve with
tacos or grilled fish, or use as a marinade
for chicken or pork. To soften the heat,
add some chopped fresh papaya or mango
before blending.

¾ cup chopped ripe tomato

1 to 2 habanero or Scotch bonnet
chiles, stemmed and seeded

1 to 2 cloves garlic,
peeled and smashed

¼ cup mixed chopped fresh
herbs, such as cilantro,
mint, and flat-leaf parsley

⅓ cup grapeseed or canola oil

2 tablespoons freshly
squeezed lime juice

¼ teaspoon fine sea salt

1 Place all of the ingredients in a blender or food processor
and purée into a smooth sauce. Store in the refrigerator for
up to 2 days.

lupita, wiping her eyes, told me i was always welcome back in her kitchen

spicy tomato marmalade

MAKES 3 CUPS

SOME OF THE BEST BREAKFASTS I've ever enjoyed were whipped up by Lupita at the lovely Dos Casas in San Miguel de Allende. When I was visiting, she would fry up fresh chilaquiles every morning, which, she discreetly mentioned, was also an excellent hangover remedy. And every morning, she would also pity my blistered feet—San Miguel has very steep streets, and my sandals were not cooperating. We spoke mostly by gesture and some Spanglish while she soaked my feet and wrapped them gently, telling me about her life in Mexico and her love of cooking— especially her homemade jams: lemon, red tomato, green tomato, hibiscus, and more. She would then point to my ears and smile at my blue Swarovski crystal earrings—a favorite pair bought in Paris years earlier—and tell me how much she loved sparkly jewelry. On the last day of my stay, Lupita made me another stellar breakfast and a tasting of all her jams. In return, just before leaving, I gave her my earrings. Lupita, wiping her eyes, told me I was always welcome back in her kitchen. Whenever I make Mexican *mermeladas*, I think of her. Somewhere in central Mexico is a hard-working cook wearing a pair of French earrings that shine like blue stars.

This is my rendition of what I remember of the tomato jam. Although it's more commonly made with ripe red tomatoes, I often make it with green tomatoes for color and tartness. It is really good by the spoonful, with grilled meats, and on hot tortillas or with soft buttermilk biscuits—especially after a long night of tequila tasting.

3 pounds red or green tomatoes, cored and finely chopped

1 fresh jalapeño, stemmed, seeded if desired, and halved lengthwise

2 cups sugar

1½ teaspoons fine sea salt

2 whole star anise

2 bay leaves

¼ teaspoon ground cinnamon

1 to 2 cinnamon sticks (optional)

1 teaspoon ground cloves

1 teaspoon pure vanilla extract

Juice of 1 lemon or 2 Key limes

1 bunch fresh mint leaves, chopped (optional)

1 Combine the tomatoes, jalapeño, sugar, salt, star anise, bay leaves, cinnamon, cinnamon sticks, if using, cloves, vanilla, and lemon juice in a large heavy-bottomed pot. Stir, bring to a boil, and then decrease the heat to medium-low and let cook, stirring occasionally, for about 2 hours (the time will vary depending on the water content of the tomatoes) or until thick and jammy.

2 Remove the jalapeño and bay leaves. Stir in the mint, if using. Place in 2 clean pint or 3 half-pint jars; let cool and store in the refrigerator for up to 2 weeks.

salad of avocado, papaya, *and* jícama

SERVES 4 TO 6

THIS SALAD IS A COMBINATION of Caribbean influences and Mexican flavors from my travels to both places. The creaminess of both avocado and papaya come to life with fresh lime juice and the crunch of jícama. Sometimes I substitute a large Korean pear for the jícama, which, although only slightly sweeter, has a similar crispness. Serve with roast pork, chicken, or fish.

2 ripe avocados, halved, pitted, and peeled

1 ripe papaya, halved and seeded

1 to 1½ cups jícama or Korean pear, peeled and cubed

¼ cup freshly squeezed lime juice (preferably Key lime)

1 fresh red or green jalapeño or serrano chile, seeded and thinly sliced

½ large red or Vidalia onion, thinly sliced

⅓ cup unsweetened shredded coconut, lightly toasted (optional)

⅓ cup chopped fresh cilantro and/or mint

Maldon sea salt or other flaky finishing salt

1 Chop the avocados and papaya into similar-shaped cubes or slices. Toss gently with the jícama cubes, lime juice, jalapeño, onion, toasted coconut, cilantro, if using, and salt. Taste and add more salt and lime juice, as needed. This is best eaten the same day it's made.

taco love: a poem

1 I choose my favorite taco truck, and, if possible, follow its whereabouts on Twitter. After leaving my lover (because I know it's been a long time coming) and drinking too many cocktails with girlfriends who are trying to make me feel better, I cry a little more and then tell them nothing will console me; but a taco might come close. I then designate the sober girlfriend to drive as I check the Twitter feed of the taco truck to see which highway to speed to with all the windows open, all of us giggling like high-school girls about to behave badly.

2 I locate the truck, go to the window, and flirt with the tortilla maker. For three to five people, I order at least fifteen small tacos. I get the *carnitas, al pastor, barbacoa, tripa,* and *lengua.* I ask for heart and liver, *cabeza*—all the body parts that ache. I bring out the shaker of margaritas and toast my friends, grateful that they will eat with me—especially the one who is on an organic juice cleanse, and the other who hasn't eaten meat in three years. I remind them how much I love them for that and more, and that life isn't worth living without friends who know how to eat the heart out of a taco.

avocado-almond ice cream

MAKES 1 QUART

IN THE SMALL HISTORIC VILLAGE of Dolores Hidalgo, in the Guanajuato Mountains of central Mexico, two brothers gather their carts in the plaza principal and sell some rather odd-sounding ice-cream combinations. When I heard about flavors like mole, chicharrón, tequila, and pulque (a funky, hazy concoction made from the maguey plant), I knew I had to meet the brothers. One of them, José, kindly invited me and my friends into his home and told us that his father, who had worked as a policeman in Mexico City, wanted José to follow in his footsteps. But after several years in the force, José quit and started doing what he really loved: making ice cream, which he hand-churns each and every day. He verbally shared his recipe for avocado ice cream, which I've since adapted by adding a bit of almond for a boost of nuttiness.

3 ripe avocados (about 12 ounces), halved, pitted, and peeled

2 teaspoons freshly squeezed lemon juice or orange juice

1½ cups whole milk

½ cup sugar

1 cup heavy cream

2 teaspoons almond extract (optional)

1 Purée the avocados, lemon juice, milk, sugar, and cream in a blender or food processor until smooth. Stir in the almond extract, if using. Chill, covered, for 1 hour. Process in an ice-cream maker according to the manufacturer's instructions. This is best served soft; if freezing for later, let soften before serving. The ice cream will keep stored in an airtight container in the freezer for 1 week.

flower and ice

WHEN I FIRST STARTED WORKING as the food editor for the launch of
Cottage Living magazine in 2004, Chef Bill Smith of Crook's Corner Restaurant in
Chapel Hill sent me a small, cardboard package. I discovered two plastic containers
of golden liquid inside of it. Chefs are often sending me things: advance copies of
their latest book, a new gourmet chocolate syrup, fresh black truffles, even plastic
sheets of stick-on spices for innovative grilling, but I wondered why Bill Smith,
a man I had not met but knew by outstanding reputation, would send me what
clearly looked like urine samples. Our intern, Rachel Beardsley, always eager to try
something new, opened the lids and couldn't stop sniffing. Then I read the note:
Here's a sample of my honeysuckle sorbet.

Rachel and I promptly emptied the vials into an ice-cream maker and
watched as the liquid transformed into a gift from the Southern gods. The first
spoonful reminded me of hot summer nights in Louisiana. As a child, I would
gather a handful of stems, suck each tip of the magical elixir, and stare up at the
stars, waiting for something Wonderlandesque to happen.

Bill has since become a dear friend and I love going out with him, a Pabst Blue
Ribbon in each of his back pockets, as we pluck sun-warmed honeysuckle from the
vines along the back roads of Chapel Hill. I try to visit Crook's at least once every
season for a taste of Bill's honeysuckle sorbet. If for some reason I'm a few weeks
late, Bill always saves me a bit of summer in the back of the kitchen freezer.

Inspired by flower ices from Arabs in Spain and Sicily, Bill created his elusive honeysuckle sorbet. He writes in his cookbook *Seasoned in the South: Recipes from Crook's Corner and from Home*: "The first bite of this tends to silence people, particularly if they grew up around here. It's like walking around at night with your mouth open." I was inspired by Bill, and since I can't always find fresh honeysuckle, I made this flower ice with hints of lavender; it would be equally good with rose petals or orange blossom. This is delightful as a palate cleanser, a light dessert, as a sweetener for iced tea, or stirred into a glass of sparkling wine, with a twist of lemon.

1 cup sugar

3 cups water

1 tablespoon dried lavender flowers (or 3 tablespoons fresh)

A few drops freshly squeezed Meyer lemon juice

1   Combine the sugar and water in a small saucepan and bring to a boil for about 3 minutes, or until the sugar dissolves. Stir in the lavender buds and lemon juice. Pour the lavender simple syrup into a heatproof glass container; let cool, then chill in the refrigerator for at least 1 hour and up to 24 hours. Strain the buds, reserving the lavender water; churn the liquid into an ice-cream maker, and store in the freezer no longer than 1 week.

just-in-case key lime pie

MAKES 1 (10-INCH) PIE

ONE OF MY FAVORITE (taco) eating partners, Sara Foster—chef, cookbook author, and owner of Foster's Markets in North Carolina—is also a taco addict. Sara and I worked together on many food stories over the years and have cooked and eaten countless meals from Paso Robles to New Orleans. I love spending time in the Triangle to visit Sara. Durham and Chapel Hill are also home to some of my favorite chefs, authors, and restaurants, including the venerable Jean Anderson, who, along with the very kind Gina Mahalek, first showed me around the area. Sara and I always have to have a meal at Andrea Reusing's Lantern, and Crook's Corner with Bill Smith, Jr., and Gene Hamer.

No matter what meal we have planned, Sara and I will often stop for a taco fix as an amuse-bouche before dinner. Once, we stopped at our favorite, La Vaquita Taqueria in Durham, and found Frances and Ed Mayes, back from Tuscany, getting tacos after their workout. Sara and I, along with friends Stephanie and Joe Bischoff, Cindy Clark, and chef Bill Smith of Crook's, all joined them, and soon we had dozens of tacos, several tortas, and ceviche spread out on the outdoor picnic table. At the end of the meal, just as Frances and Ed were debating a second workout, Sara pulled out an entire Key lime pie . . . from her bag. A "just-in-case" Key lime pie, she called it. Luckily, she's also a great workout partner.

just-in-case key lime pie

CONTINUED

The crust for this recipe is adapted from Sara's beloved Key lime pie, which she's been making at Foster's Markets for more than twenty years. Freshly squeezed juice is essential for this pie. You can substitute the more widely available Persian limes for Key limes, but please avoid the bottled juice, which lacks the freshness and tang of fresh limes. Instead of the usual meringue or whipped cream topping, I prefer a combination of fresh whipped cream, lightly sweetened crème fraîche, and a last-minute squeeze of fresh lime. At Crook's Corner, Bill Smith replaces the graham crackers and walnuts with saltine crackers and calls it Atlantic Beach Pie.

12 whole graham crackers

⅓ cup shelled walnuts or macadamia nuts

3 tablespoons granulated sugar

6 tablespoons unsalted butter, melted

2 (14-ounce) cans sweetened condensed milk

2 large eggs, lightly beaten

1¼ cups freshly squeezed Key lime juice

¼ cup heavy cream

1 to 2 teaspoons confectioners' sugar

½ cup thick crème fraîche or sour cream

About 1 tablespoon finely grated lime zest

Lime wedges, for garnish

1 Preheat the oven to 350°F.

2 Combine the graham crackers, nuts, and granulated sugar in the bowl of a food processor and blend until combined. Pour the crumb mixture into the bottom of a 10-inch pie plate. Pour the melted butter evenly over the mixture and, using your fingers, press the crumb mixture evenly into the bottom of the pie plate. Press some of the crumbs up the sides (about ¼ inch). Bake for 15 minutes, until golden brown. Remove from the oven and set aside to let cool slightly. Leave the oven at 350°F.

3 Combine the condensed milk, eggs, and lime juice in a large bowl until well blended. Pour the mixture into the cooled pie shell and bake for 18 to 20 minutes, until just set but still slightly jiggly in the center. Let cool, and then chill for at least 4 hours or overnight in the refrigerator.

4 To serve, whip the cream and confectioners' sugar until soft-to-medium peaks form. Fold in the crème fraîche and lime zest until just blended. Serve the pie with the crème fraîche topping and a squeeze of fresh lime.

tres leches & coco

MAKES 2 (8-INCH) CAKES

THIS RECIPE WAS KINDLY SHARED by one of my dearest friends, chef Adolfo Garcia of New Orleans, where *tres leches* is a much-loved favorite on the menu at one of his restaurants, Riomar, in the Warehouse District. It's based on the completely addictive traditional Latin American milk-soaked cake but with the addition of canned coconut syrup and coconut milk. Adolfo suggests using your favorite boxed yellow cake mix or a basic sponge cake recipe, such as that from *The Cake Bible* by Rose Levy Beranbaum or *Martha Stewart's Baking Handbook*. I always make two of these cakes, because inevitably word gets out that I have made them and there never seems to be enough with just one. It actually makes for a delicious sweet breakfast accompanied by very strong coffee.

2 (8-inch) round or square prepared yellow cakes or sponge cakes

2 (12-ounce) cans Goya shredded coconut cooked in syrup or 1 cup sweetened shredded coconut

1 (14-ounce) can condensed milk

1 (12-ounce) can evaporated milk

1 (14-ounce) can unsweetened coconut milk

For serving: caramel sauce, whipped cream, and toasted chopped almonds

1 Slice the cakes in half horizontally, so that you have 2 tops and 2 bottoms. Carefully spread the coconut evenly over the bottom portion of the cakes. Replace the tops and, with a thick toothpick or a chopstick, perforate thoroughly.

2 Mix the condensed milk, evaporated milk, and coconut milk together and pour liberally over the cakes. Let rest for at least 30 minutes in the refrigerator. Serve chilled, topped with caramel sauce, whipped cream, and toasted almonds.

provence

CHAPTER THREE

fig of my imagination

IN HAUTE-PROVENCE, WHERE I SPENT much of my twenties, admittedly living an extraordinary life with a loving and generous man, I was hungry to taste and learn everything I could about this new land that promised to be a place I could call home. The flavors were so new to me, and I relished the abundance of our own backyard—almond, plum, and wild peach trees; truffle oaks; linden with their fragrant blossoms dusting the pathways to my favorite fig trees, plump and bursting twice a year with heavy, milky fruit.

It wasn't uncommon for one dinner party to tipple into breakfast the next day and then lunch, supper, cocktail hour, and so on. We had guests from all over Europe and the States staying with us at any given time. It sounds glamorous, and much of it was, but as a young Asian-American woman plopped down in deep Provence—a mere dilettante in the kitchen—it often proved nerve-racking. During this period, though, often cooking for an extra ten guests at the last minute, because someone had invited a friend who had invited more friends, I did my best to hone

the few skills I possessed. And despite my lack of self-confidence, I realized that aside from an ear for picking up languages, cooking and feeding others was the only thing I could do with some adroitness.

So I read everything I could get my hands on, took Saturday classes at the Cordon Bleu whenever we were in Paris, and sought out and made friends with the best butchers, fishermen, and cheese makers in the area. Provence, in particular, is known for gorgeous fields of lavender in high summer, and market life is rich with some of the best honey, olive oil, goat cheeses, fruits, and vegetables. These are recipes I've had to adapt over the years, lacking the wealth of Provençal ingredients, but the spirit and love for that food will always remain.

the mauresque

SERVES 1

ONE SIP WILL TRANSPORT YOU to the South of France—think Bandol or Cassis, outdoor summer café tables covered with bottles of chilled rosé, small dishes of olives, and these cocktails. The anise flavor of pastis combined with almond syrup and water is refreshing and bite-y. It opens up the palate, so it makes for a refreshing aperitif.

1 ounce (2 tablespoons) pastis, such as Henri Bardouin or Ricard

½ ounce (1 tablespoon) orgeat syrup, such as Monin or Rième

4 to 5 ounces cold water (preferably spring water)

1 Pour the pastis into a tall glass over a few ice cubes. Add the orgeat syrup, stir, and top with the water.

kir provençal

SERVES 1

THESE LAVENDER-INFUSED Champagne cocktails evoke summers in the
South of France, where deep purple blooms grow abundantly in high summer.
You can also make the simple syrup using curry leaves, lemon verbena, bay leaves,
or rosemary in place of the lavender. For the perfect complement, serve with the
Lavender-Pepper Cornmeal Crisps with Goat Cheese and Chives (page 67).

LAVENDER SIMPLE SYRUP

2 cups water

2 cups sugar

3 tablespoons dried lavender flowers, or 2 tablespoons dried plus 6 fresh whole lavender stems with leaves and blossoms, rinsed

A few drops of freshly squeezed lemon juice

Brut Champagne or prosecco

Small lavender sprig, for garnish

1 To make the simple syrup, heat the water, sugar, and lavender together in a medium pot over medium-high heat until the mixture begins to simmer, stirring occasionally until the sugar dissolves. Add a few drops of lemon juice to prevent the sugar from crystallizing. Turn off the heat and let cool. Store in the refrigerator for up to 2 weeks. Strain, if desired, before using.

2 For each cocktail, pour 1 to 2 teaspoons of lavender syrup into a champagne flute and top with the Champagne. Garnish with the fresh lavender sprig.

lavender-pepper cornmeal crisps with goat cheese and chives

MAKES ABOUT 48 SMALL CRISPS

MY GOOD FRIEND LAURIE CONSTANTINO, food writer and cook extraordinaire who spends her time between a Greek island and Alaska perfecting Mediterranean-inspired recipes, kindly shared this recipe with me. These are dainty cornmeal crisps spiked with black pepper and lavender, the perfect nibble with a cocktail.

¾ cup (1½ sticks) cold unsalted butter

¼ cup sugar

1 large egg

1 egg yolk

1½ teaspoons finely grated lemon zest

1 cup all-purpose flour

¾ cup fine-grind yellow cornmeal, plus more as needed

2 teaspoons dried lavender flowers

½ teaspoon fine sea salt

1 teaspoon freshly ground black pepper

For serving: 4 ounces fresh goat cheese, chopped fresh chives, and fleur de sel or other finishing salt

1. Preheat the oven to 350°F. Line a baking sheet with parchment paper.

2. Cut the butter into about 8 pieces, and place in the bowl of a stand mixer fitted with the paddle attachment. Beat the butter on low speed for a minute or two, until softened. Scrape down the sides of the bowl, add the sugar, and beat on medium speed until the mixture is light and fluffy, about 5 minutes. Scrape down the sides of the bowl, decrease the speed to low, and beat in the egg. Then beat in the egg yolk and lemon zest; reserve.

3. In a separate bowl, whisk together the flour, cornmeal, lavender flowers (crush them to release the fragrance by rolling between your palms), salt, and pepper. Add to the butter mixture and beat on low speed, scraping down the bowl as needed, just until blended.

4. Roll the dough into small, equal-size balls using a 1½-teaspoon cookie scoop. Place the balls, 2 inches apart, on the prepared baking sheet and flatten each one with the bottom of a glass dipped in cornmeal (to prevent sticking). Bake for 10 to 12 minutes, until the crisps begin to firm up and turn golden around the edges. Transfer to cooling racks. When cool, spread the crisps with the goat cheese, garnish with chives, and finish with a sprinkling of fleur de sel.

eggs baked in cream *with* olives
SERVES 2

WHEN I LIVED IN PROVENCE, up the hill from the small village of Forcalquier, I would get yard eggs fresh from the farmer across the street and often scramble them in a double boiler with thick shavings of black truffle from our *chênes truffiers*, truffle oaks, or make *oeuf en cocotte*—basically, a fancy name for a simple delight: eggs baked in cream. The beauty of the dish is that it lends itself to so many different flavor combinations—consider basil and roasted tomato; andouille and thyme; or crabmeat and chives.

I tasted a decadent version of this same dish at Miller Union in Atlanta. Chef Steven Satterfield adds celery ribs and bay leaf to infuse the cream. And at Lincoln in Portland, Oregon, they make theirs with creamy green olives and toasted bread crumbs. I love including celery root or fennel bulb to the infusion. A scattering of Roasted Tomatoes Provençales (page 80) adds a nice acidity and textural contrast to the mix. Most important for this recipe is to use the best quality eggs and cream.

¾ cup heavy cream

2 celery ribs, halved

¼ small celery root bulb
or fennel bulb (optional)

1 shallot, quartered (do not peel)

1 large clove garlic,
halved (do not peel)

¼ teaspoon fine sea salt

6 to 8 black peppercorns

2 thyme sprigs

2 large eggs

6 plump green olives, such
as Picholine or Castelvetrano,
pitted and halved

4 Roasted Tomatoes Provençales
(page 80; optional)

For serving: toasted bread and
grated Parmigiano-Reggiano

1   Preheat the oven to 350°F.

2   Gently heat the cream, celery, celery root, shallot, garlic, salt, peppercorns, and thyme in a medium saucepan until very hot but not boiling. Remove the pan from the heat and let sit for about 15 minutes.

3   Lightly butter 2 individual ovenproof, preferably oval au gratin dishes (about 5 by 10 inches) and place on a rimmed baking sheet. Crack an egg into each dish, being careful not to break the yolk. Scatter the olives and roasted tomatoes, if using, around the eggs.

4   Strain the cream through a fine-mesh sieve into a small bowl; discard the solids. Spoon the cream over each egg until almost completely covered, leaving some of the yolk to show through; you might have some cream left over, depending on the size of your eggs.

5   Bake the eggs for 6 minutes. Change the oven setting to broil and broil for 1 minute. Turn off the oven and let the eggs sit for 2 to 3 minutes in the oven (being careful not to overcook), until the whites start to set and are no longer translucent. The whites should set, but you want the yolks to quiver. Serve with toasted bread and grated Parmigiano-Reggiano.

VARIATION

eggs baked in cream *with* foie gras surprise

This is totally decadent, I admit, but so delicious and unexpected. I make this for celebratory dinners. Combine the cream with the celery rib and 1 finely chopped Granny Smith apple in place of the celery root. Proceed with the recipe as directed, and place up to 1 ounce of foie gras instead of the olives and tomatoes in each au gratin dish before topping with the egg and cream. Cook according to the recipe directions. Taste with a glass of bubbles or Sauternes.

savory tomato *and* pesto bread pudding

SERVES 6 TO 8

I STARTED MAKING THIS PEASANT DISH, known as a panade, to use up the leftover crusty bits of *pain de campagne* and pesto from a summery vegetable *soupe au pistou*. Sometimes I add a layer of thinly sliced eggplant or zucchini. The inside is soft and rich with garlic while the cheesy crunchy bits of bread on top are the prize and quite addictive. Serve with a green salad dressed simply with freshly squeezed lemon juice and a fruity extra-virgin olive oil.

In Provence, a pistou is made with just basil, olive oil, and garlic. This pesto has nuts and a bit of heat from a jalapeño, and by itself is excellent tossed with hot pasta, adding a little of the reserved pasta cooking water if the sauce is too thick. Or chill the pasta and eat as a salad, or serve the pesto with grilled vegetables, fish, chicken, or meat. This is also good made with a combination of equal amounts of lacinato kale and arugula.

savory tomato *and* pesto bread pudding
CONTINUED

SPICY WALNUT-ARUGULA PESTO

MAKES 1½ CUPS

2 cups packed arugula

**1 cup tightly packed
fresh basil leaves**

**½ cup tightly packed fresh mint
leaves or flat-leaf parsley leaves**

**1 cup whole walnuts
or raw almonds**

2 cloves garlic, peeled

**1 medium fresh jalapeño,
stemmed (and seeded, if desired)**

**¼ to ⅓ cup grated
Parmigiano-Reggiano**

**1 tablespoon freshly squeezed
lemon juice or white wine vinegar**

½ teaspoon salt

About ⅓ cup extra-virgin olive oil

1 To make the pesto, combine the arugula, basil, mint, walnuts, garlic, jalapeño, cheese, lemon juice, and salt in the bowl of a food processor and pulse to combine. Slowly drizzle in the olive oil until well blended. Taste and add more olive oil, lemon juice, or salt, as needed. Set aside until ready to use.

2 tablespoons extra-virgin olive oil

1 large yellow or white onion, halved and thinly sliced

1 cup dry white wine

1 cup chicken or vegetable broth

1 tablespoon dried herbes de Provence or thyme leaves

Sea salt and freshly ground black pepper

1 (1-pound) round loaf day-old hearty bread such as pain de campagne, sliced ½ inch thick

2 pounds large ripe tomatoes, such as beefsteak, sliced ½ inch thick

2 cups shredded Comté or Gruyère

¼ cup grated Parmigiano-Reggiano

2 To make the bread pudding, heat the oil in a large pan over medium heat. Add the onion and cook, stirring occasionally, until softened and golden, about 10 minutes. Add the wine and simmer over medium-high heat until the liquid is reduced to ¼ cup, about 5 minutes. Add the broth and *herbes de Provence*, and season with salt and pepper; stir and let simmer for about 5 minutes. Remove the pan from the heat and reserve.

3 Preheat the oven to 375°F. Lightly butter the bottom of a 10-inch round or 9 by 13-inch baking dish that's at least 2½ inches deep.

4 Line the baking dish with half of the bread slices, overlapping the slices slightly and cutting to fit as needed. Top with half of the tomato slices and lightly season with salt and pepper. Spread half of the prepared pesto over the tomatoes, then sprinkle with half of the shredded cheese, pressing down on the layers. Add the remaining layer of tomatoes, pesto, and shredded cheese. Pour the reserved onion and broth over the cheese. Cut the remaining bread slices into quarters and place over the onion. Gently press down on the bread with the back of a spatula or large spoon so that the liquid is evenly distributed. Top with the Parmigiano-Reggiano. Cover with lightly greased aluminum foil and bake in the upper third of the oven for 1 hour. Uncover and bake for 10 minutes more, or until the top is browned and crisp and the insides are bubbling. Let rest for at least 10 minutes before serving.

six-minute eggs and *the* grand aïoli

SERVES 10 TO 12

THIS IS ONE OF MY all-time favorite ways to share food. What could be better than a huge platter of garden vegetables with a garlic-laden sauce, crusty bread, and wine? Traditionally, this dish was offered on Fridays, as meat was not to be consumed in Catholic France. Although no longer so rigid about the religious dietary rules, in Provence meatless Fridays are still common, with fish as the star. To make an even grander feast of it, consider including poached halibut or cod, steamed clams or mussels, and grilled octopus for what is known as the Grand Aïoli. Anchoïade (page 78) is also delicious to round out this Provence-inspired meal. To make the aïoli, use the best-quality olive oil you can find; for a milder taste, combine equal parts olive oil and grapeseed oil.

Anchoïade, page 78

six-minute eggs and the grand aïoli

GRAND AÏOLI

MAKES 2 CUPS

16 cloves garlic, peeled and smashed

2 egg yolks

2 tablespoons freshly squeezed lemon juice

1 teaspoon Dijon mustard

Sea salt and freshly ground black pepper

About 2 cups extra-virgin olive oil, or 1 cup extra-virgin olive oil plus 1 cup grapeseed oil

8 large eggs

3 small fennel bulbs, trimmed and thinly sliced

4 artichokes, trimmed and steamed

½ pound trimmed and blanched green beans

1 pound carrots (raw or steamed), sliced lengthwise

1 pound small new potatoes, steamed

Combination of any of the following: roasted red peppers, cucumber spears, lightly steamed broccoli and cauliflower florets, snow peas, radishes, cabbage wedges, and zucchini spears

1   To make the aïoli, in a blender or food processor, place the garlic, egg yolks, lemon juice, mustard, and a pinch of salt and pepper in a blender or food processor and process for about 10 seconds. Slowly, ever so slowly, drizzle in the olive oil with the blender running, until a smooth, creamy, mayonnaise-like sauce develops. Taste and add more salt, pepper, or lemon juice, as needed; set aside until ready to serve.

2   To soft-boil the eggs, bring about 12 cups of water to a boil in a large pot. Gently lower the eggs into the water, using a large spoon and being careful not to drop and crack the eggs. Decrease the heat to medium-low, or a low simmer with tiny bubbles. Cook the eggs for 6 minutes. Peel the eggs under cool running water. Slice in half lengthwise and set aside until ready to serve.

3   Place the reserved aïoli in a serving bowl on a large platter. Arrange all of the vegetables and soft-boiled eggs around the aïoli.

anchoïade

MAKES ABOUT ½ CUP

THIS IS A GARLIC-LADEN TRADITIONAL Provençal anchovy dipping sauce that's delicious for bread or vegetables, especially sweet, crunchy fennel and roasted red bell peppers. I like to make a big batch and have some on hand to drizzle on boiled eggs or fish, or to stir into tomato-based pasta dishes. Serve with soft-boiled eggs and the Grand Aïoli (page 74).

1 (3½-ounce) jar anchovies (about 24 fillets), rinsed if salt-packed

5 cloves garlic, peeled

1 tablespoon capers, rinsed and drained

1 tablespoon red wine vinegar

1 tablespoon freshly squeezed lemon juice

⅓ cup chopped fresh flat-leaf parsley

Freshly ground black pepper

¼ cup extra-virgin olive oil

1   Place the anchovies, garlic, and capers in a small pan over medium heat; cook, stirring occasionally, until the anchovies begin to melt, about 2 minutes. Process the melted anchovy mixture in a blender or processor and blend until smooth. Alternatively, they can be crushed with a mortar and pestle. Add the vinegar, lemon juice, parsley, and pepper to taste and pulse (or crush with a mortar and pestle) until just combined. Slowly drizzle in the olive oil. Taste and add more lemon juice or olive oil, as needed. Store in an airtight container in the refrigerator for up to 1 week.

aged goat cheese *and* spring onion salad

SERVES 4 TO 6

IN PROVENCE, GOAT CHEESE shows up in many forms: tartelettes with tomatoes and olive, crusted and pan-fried on greens, whipped into soufflés, on a platter with figs and honeycomb. For this recipe, it's best to use a dense, aged goat cheese, like a *picodon* or *crottin de Chavignol*, because it will hold up well to the olive oil. Spring onions—the bulbs that are just starting to mature—that are about the size of a baseball are also best here. I like to pile any leftovers onto warm crusty bread—the kind with soft insides to soak up the flavors—along with a few slices of prosciutto or chilled roasted tomatoes.

6 small aged chèvre

3 medium spring onion bulbs

Fruity extra-virgin olive oil, for drizzling

Fleur de sel or Maldon sea salt and freshly ground black pepper

1 teaspoon pink peppercorns or dried herbes de Provence

For serving: grilled bread and black olive tapenade

1. Thinly slice the cheese and onions to approximately the same width. Cut the onions in half again to make half-moons. Place the cheese and onion slices in a shallow serving bowl and pour over a generous amount of olive oil; season with salt and pepper to taste. Sprinkle with pink peppercorns (crush them between your palms to release their fragrance). Serve with grilled bread and black olive tapenade. The prepared cheese may be refrigerated for up to 2 days before serving. Be sure to bring the cheese to room temperature before serving.

roasted tomatoes provençales

SERVES 4 TO 6

WE ALWAYS HAD AN ABUNDANCE of delicious summer tomatoes in Provence, and this is an easy and gentle way to coax out the best flavor from the fruit, even when they are not at their peak. Use medium ripe, round tomatoes. Serve warm or at room temperature with roast lamb or chicken. These are also good chilled with fresh soft cheese and fresh basil, or simply smushed onto toasted bread. If using slightly underripe tomatoes, you might want to add a pinch of sugar.

2 to 3 cloves garlic, peeled

1 tablespoon anchovy paste or 1 to 2 anchovy fillets (optional)

Extra-virgin olive oil, as needed

1 pound firm but ripe red tomatoes

Sea salt and freshly ground black pepper

Pinch of sugar, if needed

1 tablespoon dried herbes de Provence

Fresh herbs, such as basil, flat-leaf parsley, and/ or thyme, for garnish

1 Preheat the oven to 325°F.

2 Combine the garlic and anchovy paste, if using, and mash with a mortar and pestle. Add a drizzle of olive oil to the paste. Cut the tomatoes in half width-wise. (If the tomatoes are very fat, cut into 3 slices.) Place the tomato halves, cut side up, in a large baking dish or on a baking sheet. Divide the anchovy-garlic paste evenly among the tomatoes, spreading the paste over the top. Season with salt and pepper and a pinch of sugar, if needed. Sprinkle with the *herbes de Provence* and another drizzle of olive oil.

3 Bake for 45 minutes to 1 hour. The tomatoes should be soft and caramelized. Garnish with fresh herbs and serve warm or at room temperature. They can also be stored in an airtight jar with added extra-virgin olive oil to top off in the refrigerator for up to 1 week.

tipsy melons

SERVES 4

THE FRENCH CHERISH the small melons of Provence known as *melon de Cavaillon*. I used to serve them as a first course, sliced on a large platter with *jambon à l'os* or prosciutto from San Daniele and a crack of fresh black pepper. An aging detective writer I once knew from Manosque would only eat these melons gently seeded, slightly chilled, and filled with the finest Port.

On this side of the ocean, they are known as Charentais and can now be found at many farmers' markets. Use the ripest and smallest melons you can find.

4 very small ripe melons (preferably Charentais) or 2 medium melons

Port or a dry sherry such as fino or oloroso, as needed

For serving: slices of prosciutto di Parma, chunks of Manchego or Parmigiano-Reggiano, and almonds, for serving

1 Remove the tops (about ½ inch from the top) of each melon and scoop out the seeds. If the melons are on the larger side, cut in half. Slice a tiny piece off the bottom of each melon, so that they don't wobble. Pour the Port into each melon, cover with the top, and place them in a baking dish or on a shallow platter. Chill until ready to serve with the prosciutto, cheese, and almonds.

provençal beef stew

SERVES 6 TO 8

THIS IS ONE OF THE FIRST DISHES I learned to make when I lived in the South of France. My go-to reference for food of the region was (and remains) *La Cuisinière Provençale*, written in 1897 by J. B. Reboul. There are many variations of this luscious long-simmered stew of beef celebrating the lesser cuts. Traditionally, the meat is protected from the heat by a layer of lard, and cooked in a *daubière*. Use a heavy-bottomed casserole dish, preferably enameled cast iron like those made by Le Creuset. Though not traditional, I like to thicken my daube with a bit of black olive tapenade for added flavor. This tastes best made a day in advance. Serve with soft or pan-fried polenta or large pasta shells and a simple green salad.

provençal beef stew

3 pounds boneless beef chuck, trimmed of excess fat and cut into 2-inch cubes

3 medium yellow onions, quartered

1 (750-milliliter) bottle dry red wine

2 tablespoons balsamic or red wine vinegar

All-purpose flour, for dredging

1 teaspoon fine sea salt, plus more as needed

¼ teaspoon freshly ground black pepper, plus more as needed

2 slices thick-cut smoked bacon, diced

3 to 4 cloves garlic, smashed and coarsely chopped

1 tablespoon dried herbes de Provence

1 orange

1½ to 2 cups beef stock

4 to 5 carrots, cut lengthwise and then into thirds (see Note)

2 to 3 tablespoons black olive tapenade

Black olives (such as Niçoise), for garnish

Chopped fresh flat-leaf parsley, for garnish

Polenta or pasta, for serving

1 Combine the beef, 2 of the quartered onions, the red wine, and vinegar in a large nonreactive bowl. Let marinate, in the refrigerator, for at least 4 hours or up to 24 hours. Let the bowl of meat sit on the kitchen counter for about 20 minutes before cooking.

2 Place the flour in a shallow bowl or plate; season with a pinch of salt and some freshly ground pepper. Using a slotted spoon, remove the beef from the marinade and drain well, discarding the onions. Reserve the marinade. Very lightly dredge about three-quarters of the beef pieces in the seasoned flour; set aside. (If you dredge all the beef, the resulting sauce is sometimes too thick and pasty.)

3 Heat the bacon in a large heavy-bottomed pot or Dutch oven over medium-high heat until the fat begins to render, about 3 minutes.

4 Add the beef to the pot and let brown, turning occasionally, about 8 minutes. Cook the beef in batches, if needed. Add the remaining quartered onion and cook for 5 minutes. Add the salt, pepper, garlic, *herbes de Provence*, and a strip of rind from the orange, and stir. Add the reserved wine marinade. Bring to a boil. Decrease the heat to medium-high and let the wine reduce by about one-third, skimming off the fat, about 15 minutes. Add the beef stock, just to cover the meat. Stir and cover the pot and cook on low heat on the stovetop for 2½ to 3 hours (or bake at 325°F for 3 to 3½ hours), until the meat is fork-tender. Stir in the carrots (see Note) about 35 minutes before the beef is tender enough to serve, so they will both be ready at the same time.

5 Remove any fat from the surface with a spoon. Remove the orange rind and discard. Zest the remaining rind of the orange and add to the pot; squeeze the juice from the orange into the pot. Stir in the black olive tapenade. Serve hot, garnished with black olives and parsley, or let cool and refrigerate overnight to serve the next day.

NOTE: For added flavor, I sometimes roast the carrots before adding them to the stew. Spread them in a single layer on a baking sheet, drizzle with a bit of olive oil and sprinkle with salt, and roast at 425°F for about 10 minutes. Stir into the stew 20 to 30 minutes before serving, or serve on the side along with the polenta or pasta.

fresh pear cake *with* almond

MAKES 1 (10-INCH) CAKE

WE ALWAYS ANTICIPATED THE FIRST RAW, green almonds from our trees; they were a treat dipped in a bit of fleur de sel and tasted with a crisp white wine. We used the fruit in many ways—the oil for cooking and beauty products as well as the flour for pastries. To make almond meal, whizz whole or blanched almonds in a food processor until finely ground; be careful not to overprocess or you'll have almond butter, which isn't a bad thing but is not helpful for this recipe. Alternatively, use Bob's Red Mill almond meal/flour.

2 cups all-purpose flour

1 cup homemade almond meal or Bob's Red Mill almond meal (see headnote)

½ teaspoon baking powder

½ teaspoon baking soda

2½ pounds ripe but firm pears (about 4 large pears), cored and chopped into ½-inch pieces

1½ tablespoons freshly squeezed lemon juice

1 teaspoon ground cinnamon

½ teaspoon fine sea salt

2 cups sugar

1 cup (2 sticks) unsalted butter, softened

4 large eggs

⅓ cup freshly squeezed orange juice

1½ teaspoons pure vanilla extract

½ teaspoon almond extract

Whipped cream, for serving

1 Preheat the oven to 350°F. Lightly grease and flour a 10-inch tube pan. Combine the flour, almond meal, baking powder, and baking soda in a bowl. Toss the pears with the lemon juice, cinnamon, salt, and ¼ cup of the sugar; set aside.

2 Beat the butter and the remaining 1¾ cups sugar until light and fluffy, about 5 minutes. Add the eggs, 2 at a time, beating well after each addition; add the orange juice and the vanilla and almond extracts; stir to combine. Add the flour-almond mixture and beat until well combined.

3 Spoon one-third of the batter into the bottom of the prepared tube pan. Add a layer of half of the chopped pears. Top with another layer of one-third of the batter, then the remaining half of the pears, and finish with the remaining one-third of the batter.

4 Bake for 1 hour and 10 minutes, or until a tester inserted in the center comes out mostly clean (some of the pears might stick to the tester). Let cool on a cooling rack for at least 15 minutes before unmolding from the pan. Serve with whipped cream.

fig *and* cream ice cream

MAKES 1½ QUARTS

IN FRANCE I HAD TWO luscious fig trees that offered fruit twice a year—pale green figs with coral-colored insides, and a deeper purple variety with an almost lavender-hued flesh. I never dreamed figs could be that delicious. If I didn't eat them warm, out of hand, I roasted them with red wine and crème fraîche à la Alexandre Dumas; smashed them onto toasted brioche; or sliced and perched them atop pastry cream for a fresh tart. Or I simply dipped them in sweet, butter-colored cream. This is a simple no-cook ice cream that allows the figs to be the star. Dress it up with chopped fresh lemon verbena or mint leaves.

1¾ pounds ripe figs, stemmed and peeled

½ cup sugar

Juice of 1 lemon or lime

1 to 2 teaspoons chopped fresh lemon verbena or mint leaves (optional)

Pinch of salt

Pinch of ground cinnamon

1 cup heavy cream

1 Cut the figs in half. In a food processor or blender, pulse the figs with the sugar and lemon juice. Add the herbs, if using, salt, and cinnamon. Taste and add more sugar or lemon juice, if needed. Pour the mixture into a bowl; stir in the heavy cream and chill for about 1 hour.

2 Process in an ice-cream maker according to the manufacturer's instructions. Store in the freezer for up to 1 week.

paris

to the moon *and* back

THE FIRST TIME I LANDED IN PARIS—a student, as many of us are upon arrival, wearing our hearts on our sleeves—I found a café where I was able to nurse a bottle of Perrier and a single espresso like the other patrons for a good hour or so. And in my jet-lagged state, I overheard a conversation between lovers: "But how much do you love me?" asked the woman, twirling her hair and armed with a Parisian pout I would never master. "To the moon and back," the man declared. I don't remember thinking his answer a cliché, just that I could never imagine loving or being loved that much. Perhaps out of youthful ignorance or hopeful superstition, I promptly ordered what they were having: the croque madame and a glass of red wine, imagining that certain flavor combinations would be a good start to my own adventures of the heart.

A few years later, I'd return to Paris with my own grand love story in full swing. The city was a new planet for me, full of exquisite, exotic foods, and my knowledgeable companion made sure I tried everything—brandy-stuffed livers; runny, stinky cheese; small roasted songbirds; ham shaved from the bone; wines unearthed from secret cellars—before we ventured to Italy, Greece, Spain, and Asia.

We'd return again for many years, traveling up from Provence, a place I would later leave behind, blindly choosing a heart-wrenching split with the first man who ever truly loved me. I would then go to Paris solo, where I struck out on my own as a writer, making a small living working as a translator and trying so defiantly to be *indépendente*.

Although there were other loves, and deep friendships forged, I always felt most at peace in the early mornings, with a warm baguette in hand, basket at the ready, watching the vendors set up their stalls on the Boulevard Raspail on Sundays or on other days in nearby neighborhoods.

It's safe to say that I lived for almost ten years in France and was rarely without a market basket. Throughout the subsequent heartbreaks, I learned instead to count on the seasons and always knew that a farmer would bring the best that was available. Spring, for example, never disappoints with its promise of fat white asparagus, peas and tender lettuces to braise together, yard eggs and fresh goat cheeses, and the first wild strawberries to serve with a jar of thick, cold crème fraîche. Fall is about slow braises of beef and veal, small firm apples and root vegetables displayed like jewels, truffles unearthed from deep below, and small bites full of flavor, like rich foie gras and cheesy custards that have become mainstays in my own repertoire of dishes.

croque madame

SERVES 2

BASICALLY THIS IS A REALLY DECADENT ham and cheese sandwich with an egg on top to elevate it from a Monsieur to a Madame. It's one of my first French "bites" and is available in most French cafés and bistros throughout the day and sometimes as a late-night snack. I like my egg sunny side up and on the runny side so I can swirl the cheese sauce into the warm yolk. A simple green leaf salad with lemon juice makes a refreshing accompaniment.

MORNAY SAUCE

MAKES ABOUT 2 CUPS

2 tablespoons unsalted butter

2 tablespoons all-purpose flour

1½ to 2 cups milk (whole or 2%)

¼ teaspoon salt

⅛ teaspoon freshly ground black pepper

Freshly grated nutmeg

¾ cup coarsely grated Gruyère (about 3 ounces)

Unsalted butter, softened, for spreading

4 slices white sandwich bread

Dijon mustard, for spreading (optional)

4 to 6 slices cooked ham

¾ cup grated Gruyère or Emmenthaler (about 3 ounces)

2 large eggs

Freshly cracked black pepper

1 To make the Mornay sauce, melt the butter in a heavy-bottomed saucepan over medium-high heat. Stir in the flour, and cook, stirring constantly, for about 1 minute (do not let brown). Add the milk, whisking constantly. Bring to a low boil, and cook, stirring constantly, for about 2 minutes more. Once it boils, if the sauce is too thick, add a bit more milk to thin. Season with the salt and pepper and nutmeg to taste. Remove from the heat and stir in the cheese. Set aside until ready to use.

2 Butter each bread slice on both sides and top with a smear of Dijon mustard, if using. Top 2 of the slices with the ham. Top the ham with most of the cheese, saving about ¼ cup for step 3. Cover with the remaining bread slices.

3 Heat a large ovenproof skillet over medium heat. Place the sandwiches, buttered side down, into the skillet, pressing gently with the back of the spatula. Cook for 1 to 2 minutes, until the bottom is lightly golden. Top with the Mornay sauce and divide the remaining ¼ cup cheese between the 2 sandwiches.

4 Heat the broiler to high, place the skillet in the oven, and broil the sandwiches for 1 to 2 minutes (be careful not to burn), until the sauce is golden brown and bubbling. Meanwhile, cook the eggs sunny side up in a nonstick skillet over medium heat. Top each sandwich with an egg and serve at once, garnished with black pepper.

cheese and thyme pots *de* crème

SERVES 2

POT DE CRÈME IS A CLASSIC French dessert custard, but I also love the less common savory versions to serve as an hors d'oeuvre or first course. I favor Comté or Parmigiano-Reggiano for this, but I imagine that any good-quality melting cheese would work well. Because these cook at such a low temperature, there's no need to fuss with a water bath.

¾ cup heavy cream

1 teaspoon black peppercorns, crushed

1 clove garlic, crushed

2 to 3 thyme sprigs

2 egg yolks

2½ ounces Comté or Parmigiano-Reggiano, finely grated

¼ cup hazelnuts or walnuts

Freshly ground black pepper

For serving: toasted baguette slices and endive spears

1 You'll need 2 ovenproof glass jars, such as short wide-mouthed (4-ounce) mason jars, or ramekins. Place the jars or ramekins on a baking sheet; set aside. Preheat the oven to 225°F.

2 Heat the cream in a medium pot over medium-high heat to a very low boil. Add the peppercorns, garlic, and thyme sprigs. Turn off the heat and let steep for 15 minutes. Strain the cream through a fine-mesh sieve into a bowl.

3 Combine the egg yolks, infused cream, and the cheese in a bowl and blend until well combined. Divide the mixture evenly among the ovenproof glass jars; it will probably fill the jars about three-quarters of the way. Bake for 25 minutes.

4 Lightly toast and chop the nuts. Sprinkle the nuts and pepper over the custards and bake for another 15 to 20 minutes. The custards should be slightly jiggly in the center but mostly set. Let rest for a few minutes before serving with toasted baguette slices and crisp endive spears.

celery stuffed with roquefort *and* sauternes

MAKES ABOUT 16 PIECES

WHEN I LIVED ON A TINY STREET between the Boulevard Raspail and the Boulevard Saint-Germain, about a block from the Barthélémy Cheese Shop, I always had a stock of amazing cheeses, and I went through a period of experimenting with blue-veined cheeses, including Roquefort, Saint Agur, and Bleu de Gex, whipping them into soufflés or reducing all sorts of fruits into compotes as accompaniments.

Blue cheese lovers swoon over this crunchy, rich small bite as an appetizer. Sauternes is the preferred wine for this recipe, but almost any good sweet, late-harvest dessert wine will work.

4 ounces Roquefort or other soft blue cheese, softened

1 tablespoon unsalted butter, softened

2 teaspoons Sauternes or late-harvest Riesling

Freshly ground black pepper

About 8 celery ribs, trimmed and cut into 3-inch pieces

Celery leaves, for garnish

1 Combine the Roquefort, butter, Sauternes, and black pepper in a small bowl. Pat the inside of each celery rib dry with a paper towel so that the cheese mixture will adhere and not slip out. Fill each rib with the Roquefort-Sauternes mixture and place on a serving platter. Chill until ready to serve. Garnish with celery leaves. Serve with chilled glasses of Sauternes or whichever wine you used in the recipe.

*i have since learned it's best
to drink what you like*

tipsy ham and cheese quick bread
with olives and sauternes

MAKES 1 (8-INCH) LOAF

I LEARNED ABOUT WINE, mainly through tasting, from an opinionated and charismatic Bourguignon who was also a revered oenologist. He'd visit us in Provence and orchestrate grand dinners in Paris, spreading the good gospel of what to drink with what to eat. If we had a dinner planned, he would often call an hour before to say he had just found "an exquisite and rare bottle" in the back of his cellar that he was bringing along; I would inevitably have to change up my entire menu and be a nervous wreck for the rest of the evening, hoping not to spoil the "exquisite" offering. Keep in mind, I was American and just into my early twenties going up against a Bourguignon who had at least forty years of drinking (excellent wines) on me.

I have since learned it's best to drink what you like and that there are timeless pairings that will never disappoint, such as Champagne and nerves; Sauternes and foie gras, and so on.

Although not very classic, this is one opening bite that has never failed to please even the most opinionated of palates. Think savory and moist quick bread with a boozy twist. The Sauternes offers a slightly sweet, rich, and fragrant balance to the saltiness of the ham and cheese. Substitute Monbazillac or a late-harvest Riesling or other late-harvest dessert wine for the Sauternes. Use a high-quality cooked ham with low moisture content, meaning no water added. Serve this cut into bite-size pieces for hors d'oeuvres, with small glasses of Sauternes wine. If you have any leftovers the next morning, toast the slices and serve with a fried egg on top.

tipsy ham and cheese quick bread with olives and sauternes

CONTINUED

Unsalted butter, for greasing the pan

1¾ cups all-purpose flour, plus more for dusting the pan

2 teaspoons baking powder

7 ounces highest-quality cooked ham, cut into ¼-inch cubes (1¼ cups)

1¼ cups grated Gruyère or Comté (about 7 ounces)

1 cup chopped pitted green olives (about 4 ounces), such as Picholine or Castelvetrano

¼ cup extra-virgin olive oil

4 large eggs, beaten

¾ cup Sauternes or other late-harvest dessert wine

¼ teaspoon freshly ground black pepper

Pinch of freshly grated nutmeg

1 Preheat the oven to 375°F. Lightly butter and flour a 4 by 8 by 2½-inch loaf pan.

2 Combine the flour and baking powder in a small bowl. Combine the ham, cheese, olives, olive oil, eggs, wine, pepper, and nutmeg in a large bowl. Add the flour mixture and stir to combine. Pour the batter into the prepared loaf pan and bake for about 55 minutes, or until a tester inserted in the center comes out mostly clean; some of the cheese might stick. Serve warm with chilled glasses of Sauternes or whichever wine you used in the recipe.

foie gras steamed in cabbage leaves with rhubarb-onion compote

SERVES 8

DURING MY TIME IN FRANCE, I worked with a brilliant and kind French analyst who really helped me understand that one can actually choose happiness. Years after I had left Paris, I stayed in contact with Grignon, and once we were no longer patient and doctor, we fell into a friendship based on mutual respect and a great fondness for good writing and good food. During one recent return visit to the city, Grignon welcomed me with a grand dinner at his home with family and friends where his wife cooked a remarkable meal, opening with this decadent and beautiful first course. Aside from the delicious food served forth that evening, I am also reminded of the generosity of spirit it takes to guide another human being to becoming who they really want to be.

As for the recipe itself, the frilly leaves of savoy cabbage make for a pretty presentation and work well with the richness of the foie gras. I use terrine of foie gras, which is already cooked, so you really don't need to steam these bundles for more than a few minutes. Purchase foie gras at Dartagnan.com or from your local specialty food shop.

foie gras steamed in cabbage leaves *with* rhubarb-onion compote

CONTINUED

4 large, pretty leaves
savoy cabbage

4 ounces foie gras terrine,
cut into 8 equal pieces

Extra-virgin olive oil, for drizzling

Fleur de sel or Maldon sea salt

Rhubarb-Onion Compote
(recipe follows; optional)

1 Blanch the cabbage leaves in lightly salted boiling water for 1½ to 2 minutes, until pliable. Remove from the water and shock the leaves in an ice bath to stop the cooking. Drain and pat dry with a paper or kitchen towel. Remove the thick center stem, and cut the leaves in half lengthwise (along the stem).

2 Center 1 piece of the foie gras on each half leaf and roll, tucking the leaves under, like a burrito. Tie with kitchen string, being careful not to pull too tightly. Place the bundles in a single layer in a large steamer basket (being careful not to let the cabbage touch the water) and steam for 4 minutes. Transfer the bundles from the steamer to paper towels to soak up any liquid. Place each bundle on a serving plate, remove the string, and top the leaf with a drizzle of olive oil and fleur de sel. Serve with the compote, if desired, or one of its variations.

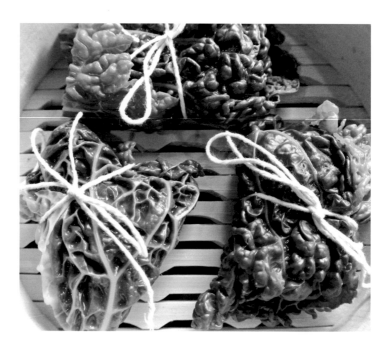

rhubarb-onion compote

MAKES 2½ CUPS

IN ADDITION TO WORKING BEAUTIFULLY with the Foie Gras
Steamed in Cabbage Leaves, this tart-sweet compote is delicious as a condiment
for roast pork.

1 tablespoon olive oil

1 cup sliced sweet yellow onion

4 cups chopped fresh rhubarb

½ cup sugar

¼ teaspoon fine sea salt

Freshly squeezed lemon
juice, as needed

1 Heat the olive oil in a large pan over medium-high heat.
Add the onion, decrease the heat to medium, and sauté,
stirring occasionally, for 5 minutes. Add the rhubarb, sugar,
salt, and lemon juice. Stir and cook on medium-low heat for
10 minutes, or until tender and jamlike.

VARIATIONS

pink peppercorn, rhubarb, and onion compote

Stir in 1½ teaspoons pink peppercorns at the end of the cooking time; garnish,
if desired, with more pink peppercorns.

vanilla, rhubarb, and onion compote

Stir in 1½ teaspoons pure vanilla extract at the end of the cooking time.
Or, scrape half a vanilla bean into the rhubarb mixture and stir to combine.

scallops with vanilla fleur 𝓭𝓮 sel

SERVES 4

I SEEM TO HAVE A LOVE-HATE relationship with scallops. I find them rich and sweet and if not prepared properly, boring; or worse, tasting of phosphates after having been plumped up by a devious fish vendor. But, when well-chosen, well-cooked, and sauced just right, they can be very satisfying. If you find scallops with the beautiful pink coral still attached, I highly recommend these. The fishmongers I used to frequent in Paris always kept the scallops in the shell with the coral intact, which makes for a beautiful presentation. Use store-bought vanilla fleur de sel or make your own by scraping a vanilla bean into your favorite finishing salt. The trick to perfectly cooked scallops is to dry them thoroughly, sear in a hot pan, turn only once, and cook just until still slightly undercooked in the center. Try these with a simple beurre blanc sauce, the Rhubarb-Onion Compote (page 101), or one of its variations for a beautiful first course; or on a salad of thinly sliced fennel, orange supremes, and olives.

12 large dry-pack sea scallops (preferably diver scallops)

1 teaspoon vanilla fleur de sel

Freshly ground black pepper

1½ teaspoons extra-virgin olive oil

1½ teaspoons unsalted butter

1 Pat the scallops dry with paper towels to remove as much moisture as possible. Season both sides evenly with the vanilla fleur de sel and freshly ground black pepper. Heat the oil and butter in a 12- to 14-inch skillet over medium-high heat. Once the oil and butter begin to shimmer, gently add the scallops in a single layer, being careful not to overcrowd the pan (cook in 2 batches, if necessary). Let cook, undisturbed, for 1 minute 30 seconds; turn and let cook for another minute. The scallops should have a golden crust and remain translucent in the center. Serve at once.

crab *and* pork spanish tortilla

A FRANCO-VIETNAMESE FRIEND OF MINE in Paris used to make this delicious egg dish, inspired by his Vietnamese mother's recipe. In experimenting, I've discovered it's not unlike a Spanish-style tortilla, the traditional thick potato omelet served in tapas bars. Fresh lump crabmeat is essential; be sure to pick through the meat and discard any stray shell or cartilage. I've found it's best to use a sturdy nonstick pan for this. In addition to the garnishes below, I also like to fry sliced shallots until crispy and use them as a garnish.

3 ounces bean thread or glass noodles

6 large eggs

1 to 2 tablespoons heavy cream or half-and-half

2 cloves garlic, minced

1 (1-inch) piece fresh ginger, grated or minced

½ teaspoon fine sea salt, plus more as needed

½ teaspoon freshly ground black pepper, plus more as needed

8 ounces fresh lump crabmeat, picked through for any shells or cartilage

1 tablespoon olive oil or canola oil

8 ounces ground pork

1 tablespoon unsalted butter

2 medium shallots, thinly sliced

Fresh cilantro, mint, or Thai basil, for garnish

Julienned carrots, for garnish

Bean sprouts, for garnish

For serving: fish sauce, soy sauce, hot chili sauce, or black vinegar with sliced ginger or shallots

CONTINUED

crab ✒ pork spanish tortilla

CONTINUED

1 Place the noodles in a large bowl and pour boiling water over to cover. Let soak for about 10 minutes, until the noodles are soft and plump. Rinse under cold water if still hot and drain thoroughly.

2 Combine the eggs, cream, garlic, ginger, salt, and pepper in a large bowl and whisk to combine. Add the crabmeat and stir. Add the drained noodles to the egg-crabmeat mixture.

3 Heat 1 teaspoon of the oil in a 10-inch nonstick skillet over medium-high heat. Add the pork and cook, stirring occasionally, for about 3 minutes. Season with a pinch of salt and pepper. Drain off any excess fat and let cool slightly; add the pork to the egg-noodle mixture.

4 Return the pan to medium-high heat and add another 1 teaspoon oil and the butter. Add the shallots and cook, stirring occasionally, for 1 to 2 minutes. Add the egg-noodle mixture to the pan and cook on medium heat, tilting the pan and using a spatula all around the edges of the tortilla, pressing the egg mixture toward the center so that the liquid runs to the edge of the pan; repeat several times and cook until most of the liquid starts to set, about 5 minutes. Set the pan evenly on the heat and let cook until the bottom begins to turn a nice golden brown and the tortilla starts to firm up, another minute or two. Keep checking the bottom so it doesn't get too brown. When the eggs are still slightly loose and just a little runny, slide the tortilla onto a plate. Cover with another plate and, holding both plates tightly, invert them so that the golden cooked side is facing up. Add the remaining 1 teaspoon oil to the pan and slide the tortilla back into the pan. Quickly use the spatula to tuck the edges under and round out the sides. Let cook for another 1 to 2 minutes, shaking the pan. You don't want to overcook the tortilla; it will continue to cook once it's off the heat. (If you are not feeling fearless, instead of flipping the tortilla, heat the broiler to high and place the tortilla under the broiler to cook until golden brown, about 5 minutes. Make sure your skillet is ovenproof if you do this.)

5 Transfer the tortilla to a large plate or platter and let sit for at least 10 minutes to firm up. Garnish with the herbs and vegetables. Serve warm or at room temperature with fish sauce, soy sauce, hot chili sauce, or black vinegar with sliced ginger or shallots.

blanquette de veau

SERVES 8

THIS OLD SCHOOL FRENCH-INSPIRED VEAL stew starts out lean—*blanquette* meaning that neither the veal nor the butter is browned—and then hits the jackpot with rich crème fraîche and egg, with a hint of lemon for a smooth texture. It can be maddening to make the first time, because it goes against every cook's desire to brown and sear, but avoid the temptation and you will be rewarded with a silky bowl of comfort food. I've added some mushrooms to the mix and like to serve this with steamed rice or hot buttered noodles. The point of this dish is its all velvety whiteness, but if you must, add a sprinkling of chopped fresh parsley just before serving.

3 to 3½ pounds veal shoulder, trimmed and cut into 2-inch pieces

3 whole cloves

½ medium yellow onion or 1 small leek, cleaned of any dirt

2 carrots, halved

1 celery rib, halved

1 tablespoon olive oil

10 ounces small button mushrooms

1 (12-ounce) bag frozen pearl onions, thawed

Salt and freshly ground black pepper

3 tablespoons unsalted butter

3 tablespoons all-purpose flour

1 (8-ounce) container crème fraîche or heavy cream

3 tablespoons freshly squeezed lemon juice

2 egg yolks, lightly beaten

Cooked rice or buttered noodles, for serving

Chopped fresh flat-leaf parsley, for garnish (optional)

1   Place the veal pieces in a large pot and cover with water. Stick the cloves into the onion and add to the pot. Add the carrots and celery. Add water to cover the meat (about 6 cups). Bring to a boil, and skim the froth as it bubbles on the surface. Decrease the heat to low and let simmer, partially covered, for about 2 hours, until fork-tender. If needed, add more water, about ¼ cup at a time, to keep the meat moist and covered.

2   While the meat is cooking, heat the olive oil in a large pan over medium-high heat. Add the mushrooms in a single layer and cook for about 5 minutes. Do not add salt or move the mushrooms around; you want them to get a light golden color but not too dark. Turn and cook for another few minutes. Add the pearl onions. Season with salt and pepper, stir, and cook for 5 minutes. Remove from the heat.

3   Remove the cooked meat from the broth and set aside, tented with foil, to keep warm. Strain the broth into a large bowl, discarding the carrots and onion; reserve the broth.

4   Make the sauce by heating the butter in a large pot over medium-high heat. Sprinkle the flour over and stir constantly for about 3 minutes. Gradually add 1 cup of the reserved broth, stirring constantly, until the sauce starts to thicken. Add the remaining broth and stir until the sauce thickens to the consistency of heavy cream. Add the crème fraîche and stir; bring to a boil. Decrease the heat to medium and cook for about 1 minute. Remove the pan from the heat and stir in the lemon juice and egg yolks, stirring just until smooth and velvety. Add the reserved mushrooms and onions to the sauce and stir. Taste the sauce and add more lemon juice, salt, or pepper, as needed. Stir in the reserved meat. Place the pot back on the stove over medium-low heat, just to warm the meat through. Be careful not to let the sauce boil or the eggs will scramble. Taste and add more salt, pepper, or lemon juice, as needed. Serve with rice and sprinkle with parsley, if using, on top.

green apple–calvados granita

MAKES ABOUT 4 CUPS

THIS RECIPE, A GROWN-UP SNO-BALL, is inspired by a tradition in Normandy of offering a *trou normand*, usually a shot of local brandy served between courses to restore the palate. Some of the old school restaurants in Paris still offer the *trou*. This is a cold and tart appley take on it; if you prefer a sweeter version, add some simple syrup to the mix. Use a high-powered juicer to extract fresh juice from the apples. This is great as is, or top it with freshly whipped cream and douse with more Calvados to taste.

6 large Granny Smith apples, cored

Juice of 1 lemon

2 tablespoons Calvados or other apple brandy

1 Juice the apples into a bowl using a high-powered juicer; you should have about 3½ cups juice. Add the lemon juice and Calvados; stir to combine. Pour the mixture into a freezer-proof (glass or metal) loaf pan or 8-inch square baking dish. Freeze for 40 minutes.

2 Scrape the mixture with a fork and freeze for another 2 hours, scraping the mixture every 30 minutes or so to obtain a grainy consistency. This tastes best the day you make it. It's also better a little on the slushy side, so make sure to not freeze it all the way. If making ahead of time, let soften before serving, and scrape the granita into serving glasses or bowls with a fork.

peach tarte tatin
with lemon-basil crème fraîche

SERVES 8

THIS IS A RECIPE KINDLY SHARED by my good friend Daniel
Schumacher. Our first meal together was at Momofuku Ssäm Bar in
New York City under the guise of an interview, which it actually was, but
between the grilled lamb sweetbreads and the puréed kimchi oysters,
we established the beginnings of a lifelong friendship based on a mutual
passion for what brings people to the table. Aside from working together,
we have since cooked and enjoyed many meals, including a classic Parisian
bistro menu at Joséphine Chez Dumonet during a trip to Paris. Somehow,
after the *boeuf bourguignon* and the escargots, we were able to devour
an enormous mille-feuille and an amazing soufflé. Promptly the next
morning we arose to seek out the best *fromagers* and tarte tatin. This is
Dan's summery take on the classic upside-down apple tart. If you want
to be more adventurous, try this with ripe mango halves or figs, or try a
savory version with tomato, thyme, and goat cheese.

peach tarte tatin
with lemon-basil crème fraîche

⅓ cup sugar

2 teaspoons water

1½ tablespoons unsalted butter, softened

2 teaspoons freshly squeezed lemon juice

Salt

6 firm but ripe peaches, quartered and pitted (about 1¾ pounds)

Pâte Brisée (recipe follows)

Lemon-Basil Crème Fraîche (recipe follows)

1 Preheat the oven to 400°F.

2 In a 9-inch heavy-bottomed pan with high sides, combine the sugar and water over medium heat, stirring, until the sugar dissolves. If the sugar starts to crystallize, add a tiny bit of the lemon juice. Increase the heat to high and cook until caramelized, about 4 minutes. Swirl the pan, if necessary, but do not stir. Add the butter, lemon juice, and a pinch of salt, stirring just to combine. Remove from the heat.

3 Add the peaches to the pan, cut side up, arranging in a circular pattern. If all of the pieces do not fit, reserve any remaining pieces and carefully slip them in to open spots as the others cook down. Cook over medium heat until the peaches are softened but still hold their texture, 5 to 7 minutes, depending on the ripeness of the peaches.

4 On a well-floured surface, roll out the pâte brisée dough to a 10-inch round. Place the dough over the peaches and carefully tuck in the sides around the fruit. Poke a hole in the center of the dough and place the pan in the oven. Bake until golden brown, about 20 minutes. Let rest in the pan for 10 minutes, then quickly and carefully turn out the tarte onto a plate, being careful of any hot caramel that might spill over. Rearrange the peach slices if any get dislodged during the process. Let cool for a bit before cutting. Serve with the Lemon-Basil Crème Fraîche.

pâte brisée

MAKES 1 (9-INCH) CRUST

1⅔ cups all-purpose flour

¾ teaspoon salt

6 tablespoons cold
unsalted butter, cubed

1 egg yolk

3 tablespoons cold water,
plus more if needed

1 In the bowl of a food processor, combine the flour, salt, and butter; pulse until the butter chunks are pea-size. Add the egg yolk and water and quickly pulse the mixture until it just comes together and starts to form a ball. On a well-floured surface, work the dough with the palms of your hands for about 1 minute. Form into a ball, cover with plastic wrap, and chill for at least 15 minutes before using.

lemon-basil crème fraîche

MAKES ABOUT 8 SERVINGS

½ cup crème fraîche

Finely grated zest of 1 lemon

1 teaspoon freshly
squeezed lemon juice

1 tablespoon confectioners' sugar

2 teaspoons chopped fresh basil

1 Combine the crème fraîche, lemon zest, lemon juice, sugar, and basil in a bowl and whisk thoroughly. Cover and refrigerate until ready to serve.

norway
and sweden

midnight sun

I CONSIDER MYSELF A SOUTHERNER—first from South Korea and then later from New Orleans. Somehow, though, just having finished studying in the South of France, I found myself in Scandinavia. Many of my friends from university seemed to be heading north; I was nineteen and so unsure of where I belonged in the world, so I followed to the Land of the Midnight Sun and caraway, cloudberry, potato, and dill. Since my adoptive great-grandmother was from Norway, it seemed like one way to connect to something familial, even if I was in Sweden instead. Much of the food there in the early 1990s, although fresh and local, was often bland, expensive, and somewhat uninspired, but there were dishes that have stayed with me, and I have adapted them over the years. Every time I eat them, they remind me of how food can bring comfort and solace in times of cold and darkness, both literally and figuratively.

swedish beet *and* apple salad

SERVES 6 TO 8

THIS IS A TWIST ON one of the many accompaniments to the holiday *smörgåsbord* that I ate during the two winters I lived in Stockholm. I prefer roasting the beets instead of boiling them as called for in many traditional recipes. This salad is also good in place of coleslaw and to top open-faced smoked or pickled fish sandwiches.

3 large beets

1 to 2 teaspoons olive oil

1 (8-ounce) container crème fraîche or sour cream

¼ cup chopped fresh dill

1 to 2 tablespoons prepared horseradish

2 tablespoons apple cider vinegar

Freshly ground white pepper

2 tart apples, such as Granny Smith, coarsely grated

½ cup thinly sliced red onion

2 tablespoons coarsely chopped capers, rinsed of salt

1 Preheat the oven to 400°F.

2 Rinse the beets and place in a large piece of aluminum foil. If they are very different in size, cut the larger ones in half so they will take about the same amount of time to cook. Drizzle with the olive oil and wrap tightly. Place on a baking sheet (to catch any leaking beet juice) and bake for 30 to 40 minutes, until tender but not mushy when pierced with a fork. Remove the foil and let cool until able to handle. Peel the beets and cut into thin strips (about ¼ inch).

3 Combine the crème fraîche, dill, horseradish, vinegar, and white pepper to taste in a large bowl. Stir in the roasted beets, apples, onion, and capers. Taste and add more pepper, vinegar, or horseradish as needed. Chill until ready to serve.

nora's cabbage casserole

SERVES 6 TO 8

MY NORWEGIAN GREAT-GRANDMOTHER, NORA, used to come and visit us in New Orleans from Minnesota. I remember arriving home from school to the scent of cinnamon and rising yeast dough and knowing instantly that something wonderful was in the works. Nora also made a simple and comforting casserole of cabbage, leftover cooked rice, and white sauce, one of the first things I ever learned to make. This is my updated version. Be sure to use the most flavorful and highest-quality meat and cheese.

1 tablespoon olive oil or rendered bacon fat

1 small yellow onion, chopped (about 1 cup)

1 pound ground sirloin or combination of sirloin, veal, and pork

1¼ teaspoons fine sea salt

½ teaspoon freshly ground black pepper

1 teaspoon dried herbes de Provence or Italian seasoning

About ⅛ teaspoon freshly grated nutmeg

3 cloves garlic, chopped

1 small head green cabbage, cored, halved, and thinly sliced

½ cup dark beer or white wine (optional)

3 tablespoons unsalted butter

3 tablespoons all-purpose flour

1¾ cups whole or 2% milk

Dash of hot sauce, such as Tabasco, Crystal, or Frank's RedHot

2 to 3 tablespoons chopped fresh herbs, such as thyme, flat-leaf parsley, or dill

2 to 3 cups cooked rice (preferably left over and chilled)

12 ounces Swiss cheese, Gruyère, or Comté, grated

¼ cup grated Parmigiano-Reggiano

1 Preheat the oven to 350°F. Lightly grease a 2-quart baking dish.

2 Heat the oil in a large skillet over medium-high heat. Add the onion and cook
for about 5 minutes. Add the meat and brown, stirring, for about 5 minutes. Add
1 teaspoon of the salt, ¼ teaspoon of the pepper, and the *herbes de Provence*. Add
the nutmeg, garlic, and cabbage, stir, and cook for about 3 minutes. Increase the
heat to high, add the beer, if using, and let cook so some of the alcohol evaporates,
about 2 minutes. Decrease the heat to medium-low and cook, stirring occasionally,
for about 5 minutes. Set aside.

3 Melt the butter over medium heat in a medium heavy-bottomed pan. Sprinkle
the flour over and cook, stirring constantly, for about 2 minutes. Add 1½ cups of
the milk and stir. Bring to a medium boil, stirring constantly, about 2 minutes.
Bringing to a boil will let you see the consistency of the sauce. If it's too thick,
add a little more of the milk. Decrease the heat to low and stir in the remaining
¼ teaspoon salt and the remaining ¼ teaspoon pepper. Stir in the hot sauce and
half of the fresh herbs.

4 Stir the cooked rice into the cabbage and meat mixture. Stir in half of the white
sauce and half of the Swiss cheese and mix gently to combine. Pour the cabbage-
rice-sauce mixture into the prepared baking dish. Pour the remaining sauce over
and top with the remaining Swiss cheese. Top with the Parmigiano-Reggiano.
Bake, uncovered, for 35 minutes, or until bubbling and golden brown.

pan-seared salmon *with* pistachio-herb gremolata

SERVES 4

SALMON IS ABUNDANT IN SCANDINAVIA, but one can only eat so much of the *gravad lax*—cured salmon—found in every home kitchen as well as on restaurant menus. This is one of my favorite ways to give a touch of color and flavor to the ubiquitous fish and boiled dill potatoes. It's such a pretty dish with the rosy salmon and green pistachios and herbs, but almost any fish would pair well with this flavorful gremolata. A fragrant bowl of basmati or jasmine rice would make a fine complement.

¾ cup thinly sliced spring onion or sweet onion, such as Vidalia or Walla Walla

1 small jalapeño, stemmed, seeded, and thinly sliced

1 cup combination chopped fresh herbs, such as cilantro, mint, and flat-leaf parsley

½ cup lightly toasted and chopped pistachios or walnuts

3 tablespoons extra-virgin olive oil

Finely grated zest and juice of 1 lemon (preferably Meyer lemon)

4 (6-ounce) salmon fillets, pinbones removed (preferably skin-on)

Sea salt and freshly ground black pepper

1 tablespoon unsalted butter

Lemon wedges, for serving

1 Combine the onion, jalapeño, herbs, pistachios, 2½ tablespoons of the olive oil, and the lemon zest and juice in a medium bowl.

2 Pat the salmon fillets dry with a paper towel and season both sides with salt and pepper. Melt the butter and the remaining ½ tablespoon olive oil together in a large heavy skillet over medium-high heat until the butter begins to froth. Place the salmon, skin side down, in the skillet and cook without moving for 5 minutes. Decrease the heat if too hot. Check the skin and, if crispy, turn gently to the other side and let cook for another minute for medium-rare or until cooked to desired doneness. Top with the gremolata and serve with lemon wedges.

creamed cauliflower frestelse

SERVES 8 TO 10

MY NEW ORLEANS GRANDFATHER was the cook in the family, but my grandmother had a few dishes up her sleeve, including crab gumbo, peach slump cake, and a more than acceptable creamed cauliflower. This is Grammy's cauliflower casserole combined with a much-loved potato dish from Sweden known as "Jansson's temptation." The addition of melted anchovies might sound strange, but it is crucial, and many who claim to detest the little swimmers end up going back for seconds.

the addition of melted anchovies might sound strange, but it is crucial

2 heads cauliflower (about 4 pounds), trimmed and broken into florets

1 teaspoon unsalted butter or olive oil

1 small yellow onion, chopped

½ teaspoon fine sea salt

½ teaspoon freshly ground black or white pepper

About ¼ teaspoon freshly grated nutmeg

2 cups coarsely grated Gruyère or Comté (8 ounces)

1 pint heavy cream

2 tablespoons finely chopped anchovies, rinsed of salt or oil

Dash of hot sauce, such as Tabasco or Frank's RedHot

TOPPING

⅓ cup grated Parmigiano-Reggiano

¼ cup dry bread crumbs (preferably homemade)

¼ cup chopped fresh herbs, such as flat-leaf parsley and thyme

1 clove garlic, minced

1 Preheat the oven to 375°F.

2 Steam or boil the cauliflower for about 15 to 20 minutes, until tender but not mushy when pierced with a fork. Drain and set aside.

3 Heat the butter over medium-high heat in a sauté pan. Add the onion and cook, stirring occasionally, until the onion is soft, about 5 minutes. Season with the salt, pepper, and nutmeg.

4 Combine the cheese, cream, anchovies, and hot sauce in a large bowl. Stir in the onion and cauliflower. Pour the mixture into a 2½-quart casserole dish and bake, uncovered, for 30 minutes.

5 While it's baking, make the topping. Combine all of the ingredients in a small bowl. Sprinkle the topping over the partially baked cauliflower. Bake, uncovered, for another 12 to 15 minutes, until golden and bubbling. Let sit for 5 to 10 minutes before serving.

warm whole-grain *and* dried fruit porridge

SERVES 6 TO 8

I LEARNED TO EAT *GRÖT*, a warm bland porridge, topped with milk and sometimes lingonberry or raspberry jam while in Sweden. I've adapted it over the years and now make it from my stash of Bob's Red Mill grains. Sometimes I make this with quinoa, pearl barley, and even wild rice; it's comforting and delicious, especially during the cooler, darker days of the year. This can be made ahead and heated up in the morning for an easy, healthful breakfast or for a quick pick-me-up any time of day. It's lovely topped with fresh fruit.

1 cup steel-cut oats

1 cup bulgur wheat

3 cups water

2½ cups milk

½ teaspoon sea salt

¼ teaspoon ground cinnamon

1½ cups coarsely chopped dried fruit, such as golden raisins, dates, apricots, and/or cherries

¼ cup light brown sugar or honey

1 teaspoon freshly squeezed lemon or orange juice

1 teaspoon pure vanilla extract

Toasted hazelnuts, almonds, or walnuts, and fresh fruit for garnish

1 Combine the oats, bulgur wheat, water, milk, salt, and cinnamon in a large pot over medium-high heat. Bring to a boil; decrease the heat to medium-low and cook, stirring often, for 10 minutes.

2 Stir in the dried fruit, brown sugar, lemon juice, and vanilla. Cook for 5 to 10 minutes, until the oats and bulgur are tender but not mushy. If too thick, add a little more milk. Serve warm, garnished with toasted nuts and fresh fruit.

cardamom-lemon pound cake *with* cloudberry jam

MAKES 1 (10-INCH) CAKE

I USED TO MAKE POUND CAKES with all sorts of local berry jams—lingonberry, cloudberry, and red currant. Over the years, I've fine-tuned the method and prefer this one, inspired by a two-step pound cake we used to make in the test kitchens when I worked as an editor at *Southern Living* magazine. It may seem strange at first, but it works, and most of all, cleanup is a lot easier since you're using fewer bowls. Use fresh cardamom, if possible; grind in a spice or coffee grinder. Serve with fresh berry jam; my favorite is the juicy golden cloudberry.

4 cups all-purpose flour

2¾ cups sugar

1½ to 2 teaspoons ground cardamom (preferably freshly ground)

½ teaspoon fine sea salt

2 cups (4 sticks) unsalted butter, softened

Juice and finely grated zest of 1 lemon

¾ cup Greek-style plain yogurt or sour cream

6 large eggs, lightly beaten

2 teaspoons pure vanilla extract or ½ vanilla bean, split and scraped

Cloudberry, lingonberry, or red currant jam, for serving

1 Preheat the oven to 350°F. Grease and flour a 10-inch tube pan.

2 Combine the flour, sugar, cardamom, and salt in the bowl of a stand mixer fitted with the whisk attachment. Add one at a time, in the following order, the butter, lemon juice and zest, yogurt, eggs, and vanilla. Mix on low speed for 1 minute. Scrape down the sides; mix for 2 minutes more on medium speed, scraping down the sides as needed. Fill the prepared tube pan and tap the pan gently on the counter so the batter evens out.

3 Bake for 1 hour and 30 minutes, or until a tester inserted in the center comes out clean. Let cool in the pan on a wire rack for 5 minutes. Remove the cake from the pan and place on the wire rack. Serve warm slices with a thick slathering of jam.

saffron-cardamom buns

MAKES 24 BUNS

THESE BUNS, FRAGRANT WITH SAFFRON, are a twist on the traditional Swedish holiday confection often made to celebrate Saint Lucia on December 13. It's believed that these were served early in the morning by Lucia herself as her wreath of candles lit up the December darkness. Make them around the holidays when friends and family drop in. I've added cardamom for warmth and crème fraîche for richness.

1 cup plus 2 tablespoons
(2¼ sticks) unsalted butter

2 cups whole or 2% milk

¾ cup sugar

½ teaspoon crumbled
saffron threads

3 (¼-ounce) packages
active dry yeast

1 large egg

1 (8-ounce) container thick
crème fraîche or sour cream

1 teaspoon ground cardamom

½ teaspoon fine sea salt

6½ cups all-purpose flour

1 large egg, lightly beaten
with a pinch of salt

48 golden raisins

1 Melt the butter in a medium saucepan over low heat. Stir in the milk, sugar, and saffron. Let cool to room temperature.

2 Pour the yeast into a large bowl and add the milk mixture. Let sit for 5 minutes, or until frothy.

3 In a small bowl, combine the egg, crème fraîche, cardamom, and salt. Add the egg mixture to the milk mixture and stir to combine.

4 Add 4 cups of the flour, stirring with a large wooden spoon; the dough will be wet and sticky. Add 2 more cups of the flour and knead on a lightly floured surface, adding more flour a little at a time and kneading until a smooth dough forms that is soft and elastic. Place in a lightly buttered bowl and cover with a damp kitchen towel. Place in a warm area until doubled in size, about 1 hour.

5 Lightly flour a clean work surface and butter a baking sheet or line it with parchment paper. Punch down the dough and knead a few times on the floured work surface to form a ball. Divide the dough into 24 equal pieces; roll each piece into a rope about 10 inches long, then roll to form a snugly coiled "S" or "8" shape. Place the shaped rolls on the baking sheet; it's okay if they touch. Let rise until doubled in size, 30 to 45 minutes. Meanwhile, preheat the oven to 450°F.

6 Brush each bun with the beaten egg mixture and place a raisin in the center of each coiled end. Bake for 8 to 10 minutes, until golden brown. Let cool for 5 minutes on a wire rack before serving. Or cool completely and store in an airtight container for up to 1 week; reheat for a few seconds in the microwave before serving.

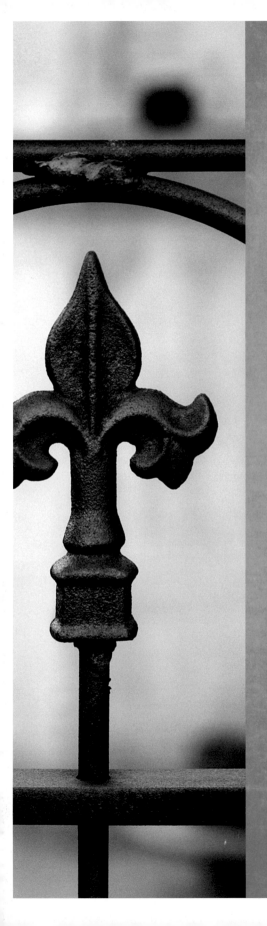

southern united states

the bayou *and* beyond

GROWING UP IN LOUISIANA, one engages in lots of big-pot meals—jambalayas, gumbos, and seafood boils—both because it's part of the bayou DNA and also often in anticipation of serving a friend of a friend who ends up inviting a cousin or two. My grandfather Poppy always cooked for at least ten people at a time. On Sundays, we'd often find ourselves elbow to elbow with a few unfamiliar faces, sometimes people down on their luck that my grandfather would meet on the way home from church. Sunday supper is based entirely on nostalgia and often leaves me longing for my grandfather's table, watching Poppy lean back in his chair relishing the moments when guests would ask for seconds.

Over the years, as I've lived in different languages and cultures, the suppers have remained big-potted, but the flavors have changed and incorporated French country classics like cassoulet, soupe d'épeautre, and pot au feu, or Italian pasta with meat sauce. Summers include a table laden with Mediterranean-style meze or Southern-accented platters of cold Spicy Fried Chicken (page 146) with sliced tomatoes, deviled eggs, cucumber-onion salad, cold sweet watermelon slices, and Fig and Cream Ice Cream (page 87).

a skin-on skirt steak that has spent time wallowing in its own delicious fat

crispy brussels sprouts *with* parsley-lemon gremolata

SERVES 4 TO 6

LA BOCA RESTAURANT, created in the tradition of great Argentine steakhouses, is one of my go-to places when I'm back in New Orleans. It was started by my good friend Adolfo Garcia and is headed up by Jared Ralls, a thoughtful chef who possesses the rare quality of allowing the product to speak for itself. Jared offers addictive garlicky French fries, the lightest gnocchi from an Argentine grandmother's recipe, and, of course, irresistible steaks, including a slow-cooked *entrana fina con la piel*, a skin-on skirt steak that has spent time wallowing in its own delicious fat.

It is mostly all about the steak, but one night, Jared sent out flash-fried Brussels sprouts. He had left them overnight in flour and the next day realized they had created their own batter, so he fried them up, and they are now a much-loved staple on the menu. The brilliance is in his recipe, but I've added a final touch of parsley-lemon gremolata in lieu of tossing the hot fried sprouts with melted butter just before serving, as Jared does at La Boca.

crispy brussels sprouts
with parsley-lemon gremolata

CONTINUED

1 pound Brussels sprouts, stems removed

1 tablespoon olive oil

½ large red onion, cut into similar-size pieces as Brussels sprouts

1½ cups all-purpose flour

1½ teaspoons fine sea salt

1 teaspoon freshly ground black pepper

GREMOLATA

2 tablespoons chopped fresh flat-leaf parsley or mint

1 teaspoon lemon zest

1 teaspoon freshly squeezed lemon juice

Canola or olive oil, for frying

Finishing salt, such as fleur de sel or Maldon sea salt

Grated Parmigiano-Reggiano, for garnish

1 Prepare an ice bath in a large bowl. Blanch the Brussels sprouts in boiling salted water for 3 minutes. Place in the ice bath, then drain well and pat dry. If the Brussels sprouts are large, cut in half lengthwise.

2 Heat the olive oil in a medium skillet over medium-high heat. Add the onion, decrease the heat to medium-low, and cook, stirring occasionally, adding about 1 tablespoon water every 5 minutes, for a total of 15 to 20 minutes. Toss the onion in a bowl with the blanched Brussels sprouts; set aside.

3 Combine the flour, salt, and pepper in a large bowl. Add the sprouts and onion mixture, tossing gently to combine and coat the vegetables. Cover and let sit in the refrigerator for a minimum of 6 hours and up to 24 hours.

4 When ready to cook the sprouts, make the gremolata by combining the parsley, lemon zest, and lemon juice; set aside.

5 Heat about ½ inch of canola or olive oil in a large heavy-bottomed pot to 350°F. Shake off any excess flour and flash-fry the Brussels sprouts and onion until crispy, 2 to 4 minutes, depending on the size of the Brussels sprouts. Transfer to paper towels to drain, and lightly sprinkle with salt while hot. Top with the gremolata and Parmigiano-Reggiano. Serve at once.

creamy zucchini skillet corn bread

MAKES 1 (9-INCH) BREAD

CORN BREAD IN ALL ITS GLORY is celebrated in the South, and as a food editor for *Southern Living* magazine, I've tasted many renditions. There's a constant debate over whether or not to add sugar. This is a version I've come up with over the years that is neither too sweet nor too savory; feel free to add more or less sugar depending on your tastes. I judge a corn bread more by its moistness than by its sweetness—there's nothing worse than dry corn bread—so pouring cream in the center is a touch inspired by the brilliant Marion Cunningham and her famous custard-filled corn bread. I like extra cracked black pepper on mine, à la Crook's Corner in Chapel Hill, North Carolina.

creamy zucchini
skillet corn bread

CONTINUED

½ cup (1 stick) unsalted butter

2 large eggs, lightly beaten

1 cup buttermilk, shaken

1¼ cups grated zucchini
(8 ounces), plus about
25 very thin slices

1¼ cups all-purpose flour

¼ cup light brown sugar

1 teaspoon baking powder

1½ teaspoons fine sea salt

¼ to ½ teaspoon freshly
ground black pepper

½ teaspoon baking soda

1 cup medium-grind yellow
cornmeal (such as Bob's Red Mill)

¾ cup heavy cream

Finishing salt, such as Maldon
sea salt or fleur de sel, or sugar

1 Preheat the oven to 350°F.

2 Add the butter to an 8- or 9-inch cast-iron skillet and melt over medium heat. You can also make this in a 9-inch round cake pan. Pour the melted butter into a large bowl and set aside to let cool but not harden. Place the skillet—avoid the temptation to wipe it clean—in the oven while it's heating. Whisk the eggs and buttermilk into the cooled melted butter.

3 Add the grated zucchini to the egg-buttermilk mixture. Sift together the flour, sugar, baking powder, salt, pepper, and baking soda in a medium bowl. Whisk in the cornmeal. Add the flour mixture to the zucchini mixture and stir to combine.

4 Remove the skillet from the oven and carefully swirl the butter that remains in it from step 2 to coat the skillet (the skillet will be hot by now). Transfer the batter to the skillet and smooth the top. Make a small well in the center of the batter and pour the cream into the center; do not stir. Some of the cream might spill over onto the top of the batter, but not to worry; it will soak into the corn bread. Place the zucchini slices on top in a spiral or circle. Sprinkle with a bit of finishing salt or sugar. Gently place the skillet back into the oven and bake for about 50 minutes, until light golden and set. Let cool slightly and serve warm, as is or with honey or jam.

coconut black-eyed peas

SERVES 6

AT *SOUTHERN LIVING* MAGAZINE, our beloved editor-in-chief, John Floyd, was always challenging us to freshen up Southern classics, a concept that has stayed with me over the years. Black-eyed peas, to me, are like the catfish of the legume family—musky and murky if not cooked properly. I've discovered that the peas lose their bottom-feeder element when cooked with a hint of sweetness from coconut and heat from chiles. Serve with Bottoms-Up Rice (page 11).

1 tablespoon olive or vegetable oil

¾ cup diced carrots (about 2 small carrots)

¾ cup diced yellow onion

1 tablespoon peeled and minced fresh ginger

2 to 3 cloves garlic, minced

1 Granny Smith apple, cored and diced

1 pound dried black-eyed peas, rinsed and picked through (soaked overnight, if needed)

5 cups water

1½ tablespoons hot curry powder or garam masala

2 teaspoons sea salt

1 teaspoon ground cumin

½ teaspoon freshly ground black pepper

1 large juicy orange

½ to ¾ cup canned unsweetened coconut milk, shaken

½ cup chopped fresh cilantro

Chopped red onion, for garnish

Chopped fresh jalapeños, for garnish

Lime wedges, for garnish

CONTINUED

coconut black-eyed peas

CONTINUED

1 Heat the oil in a large, heavy-bottomed pot over medium heat; add the carrots, onion, ginger, garlic, and apple. Stir and let cook about 3 minutes, being careful not to burn. Add the black-eyed peas, water, curry powder, salt, cumin, and pepper; stir and bring to a boil. Skim the froth, decrease the heat to medium-low, and simmer about 40 minutes, until the peas are almost tender. Stir occasionally, mashing some of the peas against the side of the pot for creaminess. Add more water, as needed, if the peas are dry.

2 Add the zest from one-quarter of the orange, then cut the orange in half and squeeze the juice into the peas. Add the coconut milk and stir. Simmer, covered, for another 7 to 10 minutes, until the peas are tender. Taste the peas and adjust the seasoning as needed. Pour the peas into a large serving dish. Garnish with the cilantro, red onion, and jalapeños and serve with lime wedges.

frank brigtsen's new orleans bbq shrimp

SERVES 4

PASCAL'S MANALE RESTAURANT in New Orleans may have created barbecue shrimp, but Frank Brigtsen mastered the dish. What you need to know, according to Frank, is this: "The dish has nothing to do with a barbecue pit or barbecue sauce." The main ingredients are fresh jumbo Louisiana shrimp, butter, and finely ground black pepper. The shrimp are usually served shells on—we like to suck the heads in New Orleans—for a messy, slurpy, spicy dish.

Frank, owner of the beloved Brigtsen's Restaurant and Charlie's Seafood, showed me how to make this classic Louisiana recipe. Originally inspired by his early days cooking at the famous K-Paul's Louisiana Kitchen around 1980, when Chef Paul Prudhomme developed a barbecue shrimp recipe that was cooked to order in a skillet on top of the stove, Frank added fresh rosemary. He later added dark beer and shrimp stock to create an emulsified sauce that is rich in butter without tasting oily. This recipe calls for serving peeled shrimp, but it is better to start with fresh, head-on shrimp so that you can make a quick stock with the head and shells. Warning: These are addictive, so consider doubling or tripling the recipe, especially to serve as a main course; your guests will leave with happy mouths.

frank brigtsen's new orleans bbq shrimp

CONTINUED

12 fresh, head-on wild-caught jumbo shrimp (preferably 10–15 count per pound)

7 tablespoons unsalted butter, softened

1 teaspoon finely chopped fresh rosemary leaves

½ teaspoon freshly ground black pepper

¾ teaspoon Chef Paul Prudhomme's Seafood Magic seasoning or low-sodium Cajun seasoning

1 teaspoon minced garlic

3 tablespoons dark beer (enjoy the rest while cooking)

1 tablespoon Worcestershire sauce

Loaf of French bread, for serving

1   Peel the shrimp and devein, reserving the heads and shells for stock. To make the stock, place the shrimp heads and shells in a small pot and add just enough cold water to cover the shells. Bring to a boil. Decrease the heat to medium and cook, stirring occasionally, for 15 minutes. Skim the froth as it boils to the surface. Strain through a fine-mesh sieve into a bowl and set aside; you will need ¼ cup.

2   Heat a large heavy-bottomed skillet over high heat for 1 to 2 minutes. Add 3 tablespoons of the butter, the rosemary, black pepper, the reserved shrimp stock, and the peeled shrimp. Cook just until the shrimp turn pink on the outside. Shake the skillet vigorously back and forth with a push-pull motion while cooking the shrimp.

3   Add the seafood seasoning and garlic and cook, shaking the skillet constantly, for 5 seconds. Add the beer and Worcestershire. Cook until the beer is almost completely evaporated, 15 to 20 seconds.

4   Add the remaining 4 tablespoons butter. Decrease the heat to low. Shake the skillet vigorously back and forth with a push-pull motion just until the butter melts into the sauce and the sauce is emulsified. Serve immediately in shallow bowls with lots of hot French bread for soaking up every last drop of sauce.

spicy fried chicken

SERVES 4 TO 6

KOREANS AND SOUTHERNERS KNOW HOW to fry up a chicken. If
you're not into spicy fried chicken, just leave off the Korean Fried Chicken Sauce.
The seasonings are up to you; some people like paprika for flavor and color, and
I love the combination of hot sauce, ground cayenne, and black pepper. At the
Seafood and Chicken Box in Alabama, somehow their fried chicken literally
sparkles. John Floyd, my former editor at *Southern Living*, says there has been
lots of speculation over the years about how they do it, but no one knows the real
secret. Another friend of mine swears there's sparkling water in the batter. To me,
it looks like sugar; to get that same sparkle, I like to top the hot fried chicken with
flaky Maldon sea salt, crushed a bit in my hands before adding.

KOREAN FRIED CHICKEN SAUCE

3 to 4 green onions, thinly sliced

6 cloves garlic, peeled

1 small fresh jalapeño or
serrano chile, seeded

2 tablespoons peeled and
chopped fresh ginger

1 tablespoon unseasoned
rice vinegar

2 teaspoons honey
or brown sugar

1 teaspoon sesame oil

1 teaspoon tamari

1 tablespoon sriracha or
gochugaru (coarse Korean
red chile powder)

SPICY FRIED CHICKEN

2 cups buttermilk, shaken

2 to 3 tablespoons hot sauce,
such as Tabasco, Crystal,
or Frank's RedHot

1½ tablespoons fine sea salt

1 tablespoon brown sugar

1 (3- to 3½-pound) chicken,
cut into 8 pieces, or 3 pounds
chicken wings, tips removed and
wings separated at the joints

Vegetable or peanut oil, for frying

1 cup all-purpose flour

½ cup cornstarch

½ to 1 teaspoon cayenne pepper

½ teaspoon freshly
ground black pepper

1 To make the fried chicken sauce, place all of the ingredients in a food processor and process until well combined. Cover and set aside; no need to refrigerate if using right away.

2 Place the buttermilk, hot sauce, 1 tablespoon of the salt, and the brown sugar in a bowl; stir to combine. Arrange the chicken in a shallow glass dish or a resealable heavy-duty plastic bag and cover with the buttermilk mixture. Cover or seal and refrigerate for at least 2 hours or up to 24 hours.

3 Fill a large cast-iron skillet about ½ inch deep with oil and heat to 345°F. If you don't have a candy/deep-fry thermometer, here are some tips: The oil should start to shimmer but not smoke, or add a small crust of bread to test the oil; it should sizzle and float and start to fry. Place a rack over a sheet pan.

4 Drain the chicken in a colander; discard the buttermilk marinade. In a shallow bowl, combine the flour and cornstarch with the remaining ½ tablespoon salt, the cayenne, and the black pepper; stir well to combine. Dredge the chicken pieces thoroughly in the seasoned flour, shaking off any excess flour.

5 When the oil is hot, place the chicken pieces skin side down into the hot oil, being careful not to crowd the skillet. Cook until golden brown on one side, 8 to 10 minutes. If the chicken is browning too quickly, turn the pieces or decrease the heat slightly. Turn the chicken and fry the other side until golden brown, 8 to 10 minutes more. The chicken is done when the thigh juices run clear and a thermometer inserted in the center without touching bone reaches 175°F; it will continue to cook out of the fryer. Place the cooked chicken on the rack set over the sheet pan to drain. Sprinkle lightly with more salt, if you like, hot out of the fryer. Toss the chicken in the sauce while it's hot. Serve warm, at room temperature, or chilled.

scrape-*the*-bottom jambalaya

SERVES 6 TO 8

WHEN I WAS GROWING UP, the men in my family were the better cooks. Jambalaya—that lusty one-pot Louisiana dish of rice and a bunch of other ingredients—was plentiful, not only at family gatherings but also on every restaurant menu and in huge seasoned pots at school fairs and jazz festivals. I didn't need to learn how to make it until I moved far away.

There's a constant debate over whether jambalaya should be red (with tomatoes) or brown (no tomatoes). I'm pretty much a jambalaya hussy; I'll take it whenever and however I can get it. To get the brown color, I know some Louisiana cooks who stir in a tablespoon or two of Kitchen Bouquet Browning and Seasoning Sauce.

When I lived in Provence, my French friends loved this dish. Maybe they liked the sound of it, or that it was spicy and exotic for them—especially if I combined pork or chicken and seafood. I hesitate to call this perfect, but when all the stars align—the wine is good and the company even better— one bite reminds me of home, and it's close.

2 teaspoons canola oil

1½ pounds pork butt, trimmed of excess fat and cut into 1-inch cubes

3½ cups chicken stock

1 pound andouille or other smoked pork sausage, cut into ¼-inch slices

1 small yellow onion, chopped (about 1½ cups)

2 to 3 celery ribs, chopped (about ¾ cup; keep some leaves for garnish, if desired)

4 to 5 cloves garlic, chopped

1 dried bay leaf

2 teaspoons low-sodium Creole seasoning, or 1½ teaspoons dried basil plus 1½ teaspoons dried thyme

1 teaspoon fine sea salt

1 teaspoon freshly ground black pepper

¼ teaspoon cayenne pepper

Hot sauce, as needed (I like Crystal or Tabasco)

1½ cups long-grain rice

1 tablespoon Kitchen Bouquet sauce (optional)

3 to 5 green onions, thinly sliced

2 tablespoons chopped fresh flat-leaf parsley

NOTE: Jacob's World Famous Andouille has been making and selling andouille since 1928. For andouille, tasso, smoked turkey parts, and more, check out Cajunsausage.com.

1 Heat the oil over medium-high heat in a large heavy-bottomed Dutch oven (you want the rice to have enough room to cook evenly). Dry the pork cubes with a paper towel, add to the oil, and cook, stirring once or twice, for 5 to 7 minutes, until the meat starts to brown and stick to the bottom of the pan. Deglaze the pan by adding about ¼ cup of the stock while scraping the bottom. Let the stock cook for 1 to 2 minutes, until evaporated. Decrease the heat to medium-low, cover, and let cook, stirring occasionally, for about 45 minutes. If the pork has "water added" to it, the meat will steam instead of brown, so if this happens, remove the meat from the pot and drain the liquid, then add the meat back to the pot. Cook for another 15 to 20 minutes, until the meat is almost tender. Add the sausage and let brown with the pork, stirring occasionally, uncovered, for about 15 minutes. Transfer the meat to a plate.

2 If needed, add a little more oil to the pan. Add the onion and celery, and stir; cook, stirring occasionally, for 8 minutes, until the vegetables start to glisten and stick to the bottom. Deglaze by adding another ¼ cup of the stock; scrape the bottom and stir. Let the stock cook down for about 2 minutes; if the vegetables have more liquid in them than the sausage you may need more time for the stock to cook down. Add the garlic, bay leaf, Creole seasoning, salt (if not using low-sodium Creole seasoning, start with ¾ teaspoon salt and taste once it's cooked, adding more as needed), black pepper, and cayenne. You can also add a few dashes of hot sauce here. Stir and cook for about 1 minute. Add the rice and stir, coating the grains thoroughly, for about 1 minute. Add the meat back to the pot. Add the remaining 3 cups stock and the Kitchen Bouquet, if using; stir again. Turn the heat to high and bring to a boil, skimming froth from the top as it boils; stirring a few more times, making sure the rice grains are immersed in the liquid, then decrease the heat to a low simmer and cover. Let simmer, covered, for 22 minutes.

3 Turn off the heat and sprinkle the green onions over the top of the jambalaya; cover and let sit for 10 minutes. If all the rice grains aren't cooked evenly, let sit, covered, for another 5 minutes. If the rice is too wet, remove the cover and cook on very low heat for about 5 minutes, then turn off the heat, cover, and let sit for 5 minutes. Transfer the jambalaya to a serving dish (so the rice doesn't overcook). Garnish with parsley and celery leaves, and serve with hot sauce.

chicken *and* andouille gumbo

SERVES 6 TO 8

A GOOD ROUX SHOULD TAKE at least twenty minutes and up to forty. I
have suffered many a "roux wrist" making gumbo over the years, but it has been
worth it. Keep in mind: The darker your roux, the more intense your gumbo.
Gumbo is always served with rice, and in some parts of Louisiana, you'll find
both rice and potato salad as accompaniments.

If it's your first time with the potato salad–gumbo combo: Serve the gumbo
in a bowl over the rice and have a scoop of creamy potato salad on the side of the
bowl. Take a spoonful of salad and dip it into the gumbo; it's a surprising and
delicious combination.

¾ cup plus 1 tablespoon
vegetable oil

1½ pounds andouille or
other smoked pork sausage,
cut into ¼-inch slices

1 pound boneless,
skinless chicken thighs,
cut into 2-inch pieces

¾ cup all-purpose flour

1½ cups diced yellow onion

½ cup diced celery

½ cup diced green bell pepper

3 to 4 cloves garlic, minced

8 cups chicken stock

1½ tablespoons low-
sodium Creole seasoning

2 teaspoons fresh thyme
leaves or 1 teaspoon dried

1 teaspoon fine sea salt

2 dried bay leaves

¼ teaspoon cayenne pepper

¼ teaspoon freshly
ground black pepper

Sliced green onions, for garnish

Chopped fresh flat-leaf
parsley, for garnish

For serving: cooked rice and/
or potato salad, and hot sauce

1 Heat 1 tablespoon of the oil in a large heavy Dutch oven over medium-high heat until shimmering. Add the sausage and chicken and brown, stirring occasionally, for 8 to 10 minutes. Remove the meat from the pot; set aside. Wipe out the pan and add the remaining ¾ cup oil. Once the oil is hot, slowly add the flour to the oil to make the roux, stirring constantly. Once all the flour has been added, continue stirring the roux until it turns a medium brown color, like milk chocolate. This should take about 20 minutes, so be patient. If you prefer a darker roux, continue stirring and cooking for another 10 minutes, but be careful not to burn the roux, which happens quickly once it turns the milk chocolate color. If it does burn, it's best to start over.

2 Carefully add the onion, celery, and bell pepper to the hot roux, stir, and cook for about 5 minutes. Add the garlic, stock, Creole seasoning, thyme, salt, bay leaves, cayenne, and black pepper. Stir to combine the roux and stock. Raise the heat to medium-high and bring the gumbo to a boil, skimming any foam or fat from the surface. Add the browned chicken and andouille back to the pot. Decrease the heat to medium-low and let simmer, stirring occasionally, for 1 hour. Taste and add more salt or pepper, as desired.

3 Garnish with green onions and parsley and serve with hot sauce on the side and hot cooked rice and/or potato salad.

down-*and*-dirty rice

SERVES 6 TO 8

IN LOUISIANA, RICE IS "DIRTIED" with crushed chicken livers and ground pork. The dish often has folks sneaking back into the kitchen for more—even those who say they don't like liver. This recipe is a great way to use up leftover rice, which is drier and firmer than freshly cooked rice and absorbs flavor without becoming too soggy. Serve with fried chicken or pork chops; as a stuffing for duck, turkey, or quail; or with a citrus-brightened green salad.

12 ounces chicken livers

2 tablespoons grapeseed or canola oil

1 tablespoon unsalted butter

½ small yellow onion, chopped

1 small green bell pepper, chopped

2 celery ribs, chopped

2 to 3 cloves garlic, finely chopped

1 pound ground pork

3 to 4 tablespoons chicken broth or water

2 teaspoons Worcestershire sauce

1 tablespoon low-sodium Creole seasoning (see Note)

¼ to ½ teaspoon cayenne pepper

¾ teaspoon fine sea salt

½ teaspoon freshly ground black pepper

4 to 5 cups cooked long-grain rice (about 1½ cups uncooked rice; chilled leftover rice is best)

Sliced fresh jalapeño, for garnish

Sliced green onions, for garnish

Chopped fresh flat-leaf parsley, for garnish

1. Rinse the livers and pat them dry with paper towels. Trim and discard any visible fat, green parts, or membrane, and finely chop or pulse several times in a food processor; set aside. Heat the oil and butter in a large skillet or Dutch oven over medium-high heat. Add the onion, bell pepper, and celery, and cook, stirring occasionally, for about 8 minutes. Add the garlic, pork, and chicken livers; cook, stirring occasionally, for about 10 minutes. Turn the heat a little bit higher and add about 2 tablespoons of the broth, scraping the bottom of the skillet. Let the liquid cook down. Add another tablespoon or so of the broth and let cook, scraping the bottom of the skillet as needed. Stir in the Worcestershire, Creole seasoning, cayenne, salt, and black pepper and stir to combine.

2. Gently stir in the rice until well combined, being careful not to smash the rice and turn it mushy. Decrease the heat to medium and let the rice warm through for a few minutes. Garnish with the jalapeño, green onions, and parsley.

NOTE: Some Creole seasoning spice mixes tend to be salty, so it's best to use a low-sodium version and then taste before adding more salt.

shrimp-stuffed mirlitons

SERVES 4 TO 6

WE CALL THEM MIRLITONS or vegetable pears in Louisiana, while others know this delicate-flavored gourd as chayote. My grandfather used to make this dish sometimes with ham or tasso and shrimp or sweet lumps of Gulf crabmeat. Years later, when I visited Les Saintes in the French Caribbean, I tasted a gratin of *christophines*, a simple and delicious dish of puréed mirliton topped with cheese and bread crumbs and baked until crisp and golden on top. Traditional recipes call for boiling (or as we say in Louisiana, "berling") the mirlitons, but I find that they taste a bit water-logged that way, so I prefer to steam and roast them before stuffing.

4 mirlitons, free of brown spots

Salt and freshly ground black pepper

1 tablespoon olive oil

¼ cup chopped pancetta or bacon

½ cup diced celery

¼ cup diced shallot or yellow onion

2 green onions, chopped

2 cloves garlic, minced

¼ cup chopped fresh flat-leaf parsley, plus more for garnish

½ teaspoon fine sea salt

¼ teaspoon cayenne pepper

Juice of ½ lemon

1 cup Italian-style bread crumbs

12 ounces peeled, deveined, and coarsely chopped shrimp (preferably wild-caught shrimp) or lump crabmeat (1½ cups)

Dash of hot sauce, such as Tabasco or Crystal (optional)

½ cup (1 stick) unsalted butter

Lemon wedges, for serving

1 Preheat the oven to 400°F.

2 Cut the mirlitons in half lengthwise and remove the soft pit, if desired (the pit is edible), from the center. Bring a pot of water to boil; steam the halved mirlitons in a steamer basket until soft and tender when pierced with a fork but not falling apart, about 30 minutes.

3 Gently transfer the steamer basket to the sink and let the mirlitons cool enough to handle. Using a teaspoon, gently scoop out the meat from each half, leaving a ¼-inch shell, and being careful not to pierce the shell. Place the meat back in the steamer basket or in a colander placed in the sink to drain excess liquid.

4 Place each scooped half cut side down onto a parchment-lined rimmed baking sheet. Lightly season with salt and black pepper. Turn the shells over and lightly season with more salt and black pepper. Roast for 20 minutes. Remove the mirlitons from the oven and decrease the heat to 375°F.

5 Coarsely chop the drained mirliton flesh. Heat the oil in a large pan over medium-high heat. Add the pancetta and cook, stirring occasionally, for 1 minute. Add the celery and shallot and cook, stirring often, for about 2 minutes. Add the green onions and reserved mirliton flesh and cook for about 1 minute. Add the garlic, parsley, salt, cayenne, and lemon juice and stir; add the bread crumbs and stir again. Add the shrimp and a dash or two of hot sauce, if using; let cook for 1 minute. (If using crabmeat, turn off the heat immediately before stirring in the crabmeat.) Add a bit more lemon juice or water if the stuffing is dry. The stuffing should be moist but not too wet.

6 Spoon the shrimp stuffing into the mirliton shells. Top each half with a pat of butter. Bake for about 20 minutes, until the top is golden and bubbling. Garnish with parsley and serve with more hot sauce and lemon wedges.

bbq ribs

SERVES 10 TO 12

A BARBECUE-LOVIN' FRIEND OF MINE in the South says it's important to cook ribs until they finally give it up and say (with the proper Southern accent): "Okay, I guess I'll go on and be tender now." The key to knowing when ribs are cooked properly is that the bone will pull out easily without the meat sliding completely off. I like my sauce on the spicier side, not too sweet and with a nice tang. Add a bit more sugar or honey if this is too tangy for you. This recipe makes enough sauce for three slabs without extra for serving; double the sauce if you like saucy ribs. If you like, after the ribs are finished in the oven, grill them for a couple of minutes over medium-high heat to crisp the edges before serving. Look for New Mexico red chile powder in the Hispanic section of your local market.

3 slabs pork spareribs or baby back ribs (about 9 pounds)

DRY RUB

1½ ounces (about ⅓ cup) New Mexico red chile powder

3 tablespoons ground cumin

1 tablespoon ground coriander

2 teaspoons ground cinnamon

½ teaspoon cayenne pepper

SPICY TANGY SAUCE

¾ cup apple cider vinegar

¾ cup Frank's RedHot sauce

½ cup freshly squeezed orange juice

½ cup ketchup

A few dashes of Worcestershire sauce

3 cloves garlic, minced

2 tablespoons New Mexico red chile powder

1 tablespoon ground cumin

1 tablespoon brown sugar or honey

1½ teaspoons fine sea salt

CONTINUED

bbq ribs

CONTINUED

1. Preheat the oven to 300°F. Line 2 baking sheets with heavy-duty aluminum foil.

2. Remove the silverskin, if desired, from the ribs; use a sharp knife point to cut into the skin and a paper towel to grab the skin and remove.

3. To make the rub, combine all of the rub ingredients in a bowl and massage it into the ribs on both sides evenly. Bake, uncovered, for 2 hours.

4. To make the sauce, combine all of the sauce ingredients in a medium saucepan over medium heat, and cook, stirring occasionally, for about 15 minutes. After the ribs have cooked for 2 hours, brush the ribs with the sauce. Wrap the ribs tightly in aluminum foil and bake for 1 hour more, or until the meat is tender and the bone pulls easily out of the meat. Unwrap and serve at once with more sauce on the side.

buttermilk-cherry-balsamic ice cream

MAKES ABOUT 1½ QUARTS

SOUTHERNERS LOVE BUTTERMILK and use it in everything from fried chicken to salad dressings to cakes. A friend of mine from Alabama told me that one of her favorite childhood snacks was crumbling stale leftover corn bread into a cold glass of buttermilk and eating it with a spoon. This ice cream is a delicious, tangy, no-cook treat. You can always change up the fruit, depending on what's in season. I often make this with fresh peaches, scraped vanilla beans, and sometimes fresh basil leaves. I added balsamic vinegar on a whim to the cherries in this recipe and really love the slight earthy hint it offers.

14 ounces cherries, pitted

1½ cups buttermilk, shaken

1 cup heavy cream

1 cup sugar

¼ teaspoon fine sea salt

½ teaspoon freshly squeezed lemon juice

½ vanilla bean or ½ teaspoon pure vanilla extract

1 to 2 teaspoons good-quality thick balsamic vinegar (optional)

1 Purée the cherries in a food processor (this should yield about 1¼ cups). Pour the cherries into a large bowl; add the buttermilk, cream, sugar, salt, and lemon juice. Scrape the vanilla seeds into the mixture, or stir in the vanilla extract, and add the balsamic vinegar, if using. Stir to combine. Chill for at least 1 hour in the refrigerator.

2 Process in an ice-cream maker according to the manufacturer's instructions. This ice cream will keep frozen for up to 1 week.

triple layer chocolate-coconut cake

MAKES 1 (8-INCH) LAYER CAKE

GERMAN CHOCOLATE CAKE WAS a standard at Oktoberfests and Lutheran gatherings when I was growing up. After some research, I realized that many of those recipes call for boxed cake mix and canned frosting. I wanted to experiment and come up with something a little less prefab and with a deeper chocolate flavor. While I was thinking about this cake, I couldn't help but remember Tom Douglas's creamy, billowy triple-coconut cream pie from Dahlia Bakery in Seattle and Ann Amernick's chocolate cake that I tasted years ago when she was pastry chef at Palena Restaurant in Washington, D.C., both of which have influenced this super-moist and tender version layered with vanilla-flecked coconut pastry cream. It's the best German chocolate cake meets coconut cream pie. There's no doubt that this is a special cake that requires some time and organization, but every bite will remind you it was worth the effort. The flavor is enhanced after a day or two in the refrigerator, so make sure to keep a slice or two tucked away.

triple layer
chocolate-coconut cake

CONTINUED

2 cups sugar

1¼ cups cake flour

1¼ cups unsweetened natural
cocoa powder (not Dutch-process)

2 teaspoons baking soda

1½ teaspoons baking powder

¼ teaspoon salt

1 cup buttermilk, shaken
(low-fat is fine)

3 large eggs

¾ cup room temperature water

¼ cup heavy cream

1 to 2 teaspoons pure
vanilla extract

4 tablespoons unsalted
butter, melted and cooled
to room temperature

COCONUT
PASTRY CREAM

¾ cup (1½ sticks) unsalted butter

2 cups whole milk

1 cup sugar

1 vanilla bean, split lengthwise

6 egg yolks

2½ cups shredded unsweetened
coconut, plus 1 cup for topping

1. Preheat the oven to 350°F. Butter three 8-inch round cake pans and cut out rounds with parchment paper to line the pans; butter the paper.

2. Sift together the sugar, flour, cocoa powder, baking soda, baking powder, and salt into a large bowl.

3. Whisk together the buttermilk, eggs, water, cream, and vanilla in a medium bowl until just combined. Add the buttermilk mixture to the flour mixture, and whisk until smooth, scraping down the sides of the bowl with a rubber spatula. Add the melted butter, and whisk until well-combined. The batter will be thin. Divide the batter evenly among the prepared pans, gently shaking the pans to even out the batter, if necessary.

4. Bake for 18 to 20 minutes, until the cakes start to pull away from the sides of the pan and a tester inserted in the center comes out clean. Let the cakes cool in the pans on cooling racks for 10 minutes; then invert onto the racks to remove the cakes. The cakes can be made 1 day ahead. Let cool completely before wrapping in plastic wrap.

5. To make the pastry cream, combine the butter, milk, and sugar in a medium saucepan over medium-high heat; scrape the vanilla bean and add the seeds and both halves to the pan; bring to a boil. Decrease the heat to low and simmer for 1 minute. Whisk together the egg yolks in a large bowl until just combined. Whisk about 1 cup of the hot milk mixture into the yolks to temper them, then pour the yolk mixture into the saucepan. Cook, whisking often, over medium heat until slightly thickened, about 2 minutes. Remove from the heat, remove and discard the vanilla bean halves, and whisk in the coconut—don't worry, stirring (and later chilling) will thicken the cream to a custard-like consistency. Pour into a shallow bowl. Let cool; cover and refrigerate until chilled (up to 24 hours).

6 To assemble the cake, place 1 layer on a cake plate. Spread with one-third of the chilled pastry cream. Repeat with the remaining layers and remaining pastry cream. Top the cake with the remaining 1 cup coconut, pressing it gently into the top layer of pastry cream. Cover with a cake dome or loosely with plastic wrap and refrigerate until ready to serve.

king cake royale

MAKES 2 LARGE CAKES

MY FRIEND CATIE CAPONETTO is a brilliant scientist as well as baker extraordinaire. For Mardi Gras and New Orleans Saints parties or whenever we were feeling a longing for the Big Easy, Catie would make this twist on a traditional king cake, which is less of a cake and more like a yeast roll. We wondered what the cake would taste like with almond paste and an almond glaze. The result is a light, tender yeast bread that's not too sweet.

According to some traditions, a plastic baby is hidden inside each king cake, and the person who receives the slice with the baby is crowned the "king" or "queen" and must buy or make the next king cake. Packets of plastic baby party favors can be found at most craft stores. To achieve this, one plastic baby is gently tucked into each cake at the beginning of the rolling process.

1 (16-ounce) container sour cream

⅓ cup plus 1 tablespoon granulated sugar

4 tablespoons unsalted butter

1 teaspoon salt

2 (¼-ounce) packages active dry yeast

½ cup warm water (100° to 110°F)

2 large eggs, lightly beaten

6 to 6½ cups bread flour or all-purpose flour

ALMOND FILLING

½ cup confectioners' sugar

1 (8-ounce) package cream cheese, softened

1 (7-ounce) package almond paste, crumbled

1 large egg

1 teaspoon pure vanilla extract

1 teaspoon finely grated orange zest

ALMOND GLAZE

3 cups confectioners' sugar

3 tablespoons unsalted butter, melted

5 tablespoons freshly squeezed orange juice

¼ teaspoon almond extract

2 tablespoons milk

GARNISH

1 cup almond slices, toasted

White or purple, gold, and green sparkling sugar

1 Place the sour cream, ⅓ cup of the granulated sugar, the butter, and salt together in a medium saucepan over low heat, stirring often until the butter melts. Set aside and let cool to 100° to 110°F.

2 Stir the yeast, warm water, and the remaining 1 tablespoon granulated sugar together in a 1-cup glass measuring cup, and let stand for 5 minutes.

3 Beat the sour cream mixture, yeast mixture, the eggs, and 2 cups of the flour on medium speed with a stand mixer fitted with the dough hook until smooth. Decrease the speed to low, and gradually add enough additional flour (4 to 4½ cups) until a soft dough forms. Turn the dough out onto a lightly floured surface, and knead until smooth and elastic, 8 to 10 minutes. Place the dough in a well-greased bowl. Cover and let rise in a warm, draft-free place for 1 hour, or until the dough doubles in size.

4 To make the filling, beat all of the ingredients together in a large bowl on medium speed with a stand mixer. The filling may be a bit lumpy. Punch down the dough and divide it in half. Roll each portion into a 12 by 20-inch rectangle. Divide the filling evenly over each dough rectangle, leaving 1-inch borders all around.

5 To assemble, line 2 baking sheets with parchment paper, or lightly grease them. Roll up each dough rectangle in a jelly-roll fashion, starting at one long side. (If including the plastic babies, tuck one in each cake at the beginning of the rolling process so they will each be positioned deep within the cakes.) Place each dough roll, seam side down, on a prepared baking sheet. Bring the ends of each roll together to form an oval ring, moistening and pinching the edges together to seal. Cover and let rise in a warm, draft-free place for 20 to 30 minutes, until doubled in size. Meanwhile, preheat the oven to 375°F.

6 Bake the cakes, rotating the pans after 10 minutes, for 20 to 23 minutes, until golden brown. Lightly toast the almond slices while the cakes bake. Cool the cakes slightly, preferably on wire racks, for about 5 minutes.

7 To make the glaze, combine all of the ingredients in a medium bowl, stirring to blend well. Drizzle the glaze over the warm cakes. Sprinkle with the decorating sugars and toasted almond slices. Let cool completely before serving.

italy

super tuscans

ENZO, A CORTONESE CAB DRIVER, has guided me out of the Florence airport and into his car. We are speeding along steep and narrow passageways, toward the town of Cortona. Enzo's Italian is almost as fast as his Fiat as he points out eleventh-century forts and medieval castles along the way. "It's very hot here, yes? 39 degrees, over 100 Fahrenheit." I think it was 62 Fahrenheit and stormy when I left Anchorage about 24 hours ago. "Where you come from?" he finally asks, looking into the rearview mirror and slowing down a bit.

I explain—in my rumble-tumble Italian with a few French words thrown in, along with a hand gesture—that I am from New Orleans but that I've just flown 10,000 miles from Anchorage to Florence. I don't mention that I was just in Emilia-Romagna two weeks ago to write about prosciutto and Parmigiano-Reggiano for a glossy custom publication before heading back to Anchorage and flying out again to come here, to Tuscany. I don't know how to say in his language that I have given up trying to understand which time zone I am in.

"Alaska?" Enzo looks confused. "Ah, Mount McKinley. Sal-mon. *Va bene*, but," as if offering condolences, he says, "it is not Italia." I know it is not Italia. Nothing is like Italia, but the man I think I love is in Alaska. After an hour or so, Enzo stops the car. "Ohh kay," he says. "We arrive. There is Eduardo."

I find myself at the entrance to a crowded Italian food shop, where a wine tasting is going on. Ed Mayes, poet and host extraordinaire, tall and lean with spiky silver hair, is much more handsome and charismatic than his character in the film version of *Under the Tuscan Sun*. Ed greets me with a kiss on the cheeks *all'italiano*.

"So glad you're here!"

Robert, a Washington, D.C.–based author and journalist that Ed introduces me to, welcomes me warmly, hurries to arrange my luggage into a secure spot, and then takes his place behind a counter full of open wine bottles. Robert's cheeks are flushed

and bright and I am instantly charmed by this person, who has happily rolled up his Washington sleeves in favor of pouring wines here in Cortona.

"Try this one," he insists, holding up a glass of white Pinot Bianco. "Frances and Ed and I just got back from Friuli."

I thank him and place the coolness of the glass for an instant against my cheek. I make my way through the shelves filled with dried porcini mushrooms, fresh and aged cheeses, and packages of Old World flavors I can already taste, like chocolate sponge cake soaked in Vin Santo.

Everyone seems happy, gesturing and chatting, dressed impeccably for a late summer Tuscan party. I spot *la bella* Francesca: the reason I have come to Cortona. She is glowing but a bit exhausted from days of festivities, mainly celebrating the twentieth anniversary of Bramasole, her home, which she labored over for many years and later made famous in her books about Tuscany. I haven't seen her and Ed since a visit to their other home, in North Carolina, almost a year ago.

She greets me warmly and wonders how I'm still standing after such a long journey. "I'm in Italia . . . with you and Ed and all . . . this. How could I possibly sleep?"

There are about fifteen of us, and we eventually head toward a restaurant above the piazza. I haven't slept in almost two days, and I don't know if I'm more hungry or tired. Robert pours me a glass of red and nods for me to try it.

"Like me," I assure him after one swirl. "A bit barnyardy."

He smiles, and I think I hear him say, "That's hot." Flirting here is part of the DNA; everyone from waiters to songbirds know how to make you feel loved. If you're not Italian, it comes naturally the minute you are seated at the table.

How could you not feel sexy passing around platters of fat figs with fresh pecorino and reaching over one another for a taste of *crostini di fegatini*, chicken liver crushed with capers and vinegar on warm bread? Later, we share plump ravioli stuffed with sweet cabbage and summer truffles. There is also wine and more wine.

"So tell me, what in the world are you doing in Anchorage?" Frances asks, offering up her glass to toast my arrival and the long workweek ahead of us.

"Obviously a love interest," Robert offers up, half teasing.

"Obviously," I concur. In my exhausted state, I refrain from telling Frances just yet about my reluctance to be in Alaska, so far from anything I've ever known.

"But," Ed asks, getting down to what is essential. "How's the food in Anchorage?"

"Well, there's an abundance of salmon and delicious oysters . . . from some bay called Catch-ama-something . . . and. . . ." I look down at my plate of fragrant summer fruit, whipped fresh cheese, prosciutto, and bresaola. I can't lie. Ed and Frances know what good food means to me—something much more than sustenance—and Alaska is not known for its culinary gems, although there are many inspiring home cooks I'm fortunate to have met.

Someone mentions baked Alaska, and there is laughter and more *vino*. I take another sip from my glass and remind myself to be here, in the moment. In Italia, sitting between Frances and Ed, delighted that the wine is flowing, coursing though my blood at an alarmingly high speed. I kick off my shoes and watch the last light disappear behind the balconies of the piazza as I bite into the sweetest melon I have ever tasted.

The next morning I am up way too early, not knowing what country I'm in or which language I'm supposed to speak. I open the window to the sound of water sprinklers and unfamiliar birdsong, the woody scent of thyme and santolina. I find my way downstairs to see Robert sprawled out on the Diane Lane bed from the film version of *Under the Tuscan Sun*. I tiptoe by, but not quietly enough.

"What time is it?" he grumbles. "How much wine did we drink?"

"I think it's 5 or 6 A.M. here," I say, shielding my eyes. "I'm sorry if I woke you. I can't sleep."

He mumbles something under his breath, eyes still closed. I stand and wait for him to stir again. "Okay, okay," he finally says. "I'll get up. Let me shower and we'll go into town."

I do a little hop and skip, grateful to this man who has taken pity on me, jet-lagged vagabond that I am. Once in Cortona, we find an outdoor café and Robert enjoys chatting with the waiters in Italian before finally ordering *ristretto*, short espresso. I tell him that I am craving something salty. He indulges me and we finally find a small pizzeria with signs of life. Robert keeps circling, telling me not to be the first hovering at the doorway. "It's barely noon. We don't want to be taken for American *turisti*."

I love watching the oversize women in their spotted aprons, tiny sweat beads above their lip line. I suddenly want to be one of them pulling out the first batches of warm dough. One of the women finally nods for me to come in and offers a slice of her lovingly crafted pizza topped with torn mozzarella, basil, tomato—*la bella* Margherita, the true queen of them all.

I tell the woman in some gumbo of a language that her pizza is better than melatonin or Klonopin; a much better cure for jet lag, insomnia, and even heartbreak. Robert can't help himself either. Once he has taken a bite, he is smitten. We spin

around on the stools like happy kids, tomato sauce dripping down our chins, ribbing one another at how *buona* our fortune is.

The rest of the week will prove just as *buona*, as I will help make dozens of pizzas for a party later in the afternoon and then cook with Frances for her upcoming book, *The Tuscan Sun Cookbook*. Among other recipes, we will make whole veal shin (*stinco di vitello*), hazelnut gelato, and baked semolina gnocchi to be photographed by her friend, Steven Rothfeld. It is fun to be in the kitchen of this Little Red Riding Hood of a house and cooking together, but also exhausting. Luckily, everyone pitches in. Susan scrubs dishes and chops *odori*, herbs. Ed pops in with a basket of freshly cut lettuces from the garden, and to fry up squash blossoms and *fritto misto* of fresh sardines, calamari, thin slices of lemon. We are mesmerized as Gilda, a much-loved local home cook, whisks persimmon-colored egg yolks and flour into large ravioli.

Frances and I are giddy with fatigue and giggle at the name of our *stinco* (which doesn't stink at all) while she tells me of an American friend who pronounces *gnocchi* as "nooky." So we whip up *stinco* and "nooky" and finally find a moment to rest at a table under the stars. Later, when I tell Neil about the constellations, he'll remind me that I've been in Alaska most of the summer, with a night sky distorted by midnight sun. I won't tell him how I've missed dark nights bursting with points of light.

We sit for a moment in silence and watch the june bugs jazz about. We marvel

so we whip up stinco and "nooky" and finally find a moment to rest at a table under the stars

at Ed's commitment to writing a poem a day, and the exquisite taste of Friulian wine. We make it back to my favorite subject: How Frances was struck with love like lightning, and how grateful she is for her life, taking nothing for granted. I admire her generosity and grace, the ease with which she becomes this landscape.

I already sense that Alaska is not my landscape, but at this point in my life, it's not so much about the place as it is about the people. In this case, the person. And while not wanting to settle, meeting Neil has made me wish to be settled.

Ed turns up the volume of the iPod player and our words give way to the three tenors belting out "Nessun Dorma." None shall sleep. Slowly, as if in a dream, we leave the table, bidding one another the sweetest of slumbers. I watch Ed, tender and gentle, as

he guides Frances to rest, and wonder if I will ever be so lucky to be struck with love.

Nessun dorma. How could anyone sleep with all the promise of love abuzz like butterflies, and the endless combination of flavors and colors and light of this region? I would rather spend a thousand days and nights awake and on my feet rolling out ravioli, rubbing down *stinco* with garlic, herbs, and citrus, and drinking under the stars than succumbing to a few nights of overrated sleep.

I gather the empty bottles and glasses and step barefoot into the cool grass, back toward the kitchen, and stop for a moment to take in the sounds of the mountain at night. I open my mouth one last time to take in deep gulps of Italian sky and wind, swallowing whole this endless spray of summer stars. There's so much still to taste and discover and learn, here and beyond. My work has just begun.

grilled peaches
wrapped in prosciutto

MAKES 40 PIECES

MANY ITALIAN MEALS START with an antipasti platter of salt-cured ham and seasonal fruit. In summer, I like how salty-sweet prosciutto crisps up nicely when grilled and makes for a delicious bite of summer with ripe peaches. You can also offer this easy hors d'oeuvre as a starter with creamy burrata cheese and arugula dressed lightly with olive oil and lemon juice. If you don't like the fuzz, peel the peaches before wrapping in prosciutto.

4 ripe but firm peaches, each cut into 8 to 10 slices, depending on size of peach

20 thinly sliced pieces of prosciutto di Parma, cut in half lengthwise to make 40 thin slices

Maldon sea salt or other finishing salt

Freshly ground black pepper

1 Heat a grill to medium-high. Wrap each peach slice with a slice of prosciutto and grill the wrapped peaches, turning once, for 1 to 2 minutes total. The prosciutto should be just crispy but not brittle. Alternatively, you can broil these in the oven, watching carefully to prevent burning, for a minute or two, until the prosciutto is crispy. Season with a little pepper to taste. Serve warm.

crushed chicken liver crostini

SERVES 6 TO 8

CROSTINI DI FEGATINI IS A CLASSIC Tuscan appetizer, and the best rendition I've tasted is offered at the third-generation, family-run Cammillo Trattoria in the Oltrarno district of Florence, one of my favorite places to dine in the city. Both the bread and the crushed chicken livers are served warm, and I often order the crostini along with a bowl of white cannellini beans peppered with green olive oil, and, if in season, fried zucchini blossoms, before moving on to the pasta. I wouldn't say the anchovy here is essential, but it would be a shame to omit it.

1 pound chicken livers

1 tablespoon olive oil

1 tablespoon unsalted butter

1 shallot, chopped

2 cloves garlic, peeled

Sea salt and freshly ground black pepper

Pinch of red pepper flakes

¼ cup dry red wine

1 tablespoon capers, rinsed

1 to 2 anchovy fillets

1 baguette or pain de campagne, sliced

1 Rinse the livers and pat them dry with paper towels. Trim and discard any visible fat, green parts, or membrane; set aside. Heat the olive oil and butter over medium-high heat in a large sauté pan until frothy. Add the shallot and cook, stirring occasionally, for about 2 minutes. Add the chicken livers and garlic and stir. Season with salt, pepper, and crushed red pepper flakes to taste.

2 Turn the heat to high and add the red wine, stirring, until some of the alcohol evaporates, about 1 minute. Turn off the heat. The livers should be just pink in the center; you don't want to overcook or the livers will get tough. Stir in the capers and anchovy. Let cool slightly.

3 Pulse the mixture in a food processor until well blended but still a bit chunky. Toast the bread slices and serve warm with the chicken liver spread.

mini meatballs two ways

SERVES 4 TO 6

MY FIRST STOP IN ITALY is usually Florence, to visit some old friends hanging in the Uffizi Gallery and then off to dine at my favorite trattorias, markets, and gelaterias. Near the Mercato di Sant'Ambrogio, I had the most tender and airy meatballs at the Teatro del Sale, run by the charismatic Fabio Picchi and his wife, Maria Cassi. After several attempts, he finally whispered the secret to his meatballs: "Creamy mashed potato to give them life, and maybe . . . a little bread soaked in milk. . . ." For a more overall airy texture, I like to grate the cheese with a Microplane, and to change up the flavor, I sometimes add toasted pine nuts and a handful of currants to the mix. At the Teatro del Sale, Fabio serves these with capers and anchovies, which I love, but for the anchovy averse, I also offer a simple, fresh tomato sauce.

1 (8-ounce) russet or Yukon gold potato or ½ cup leftover light and creamy mashed potatoes

2 tablespoons unsalted butter

1 to 2 tablespoons milk or cream

1 pound ground pork or combination of ground pork, beef, and veal

1 large egg

¼ cup grated Parmigiano-Reggiano

⅛ cup fine dry bread crumbs

1 large clove garlic, minced

1 teaspoon fine sea salt

½ teaspoon freshly ground black pepper

¼ cup toasted pine nuts (optional)

2 tablespoons dried currants (optional)

1 tablespoon olive oil

Anchovy-Caper Sauce (recipe follows) or Fresh Tomato Sauce (recipe follows)

1 If making fresh mashed potato, boil the potato in lightly salted water until tender. Drain, peel, and mash the potato while still warm. Add 1 tablespoon of the butter and 1 tablespoon of the milk. If the potatoes are dry, add another tablespoon of milk; whip until light and airy. In a separate bowl, combine the ground meat, egg, cheese, bread crumbs, garlic, salt, and pepper. (If adding pine nuts or currants, as mentioned in the headnote, add here.) Add the egg-meat mixture to the potato and stir just to combine; you don't want to overwork the mixture. Roll into small meatballs (1 to 1½ inches).

2 Heat the remaining 1 tablespoon butter and the olive oil in a large skillet over medium-high heat. Cook the meatballs in 2 batches, turning once or twice, until tender and cooked through, about 8 minutes. Transfer to a platter lined with paper towels. Serve warm with either or both sauces.

CONTINUED

mini meatballs two ways
CONTINUED

anchovy-caper sauce
MAKES ABOUT ⅓ CUP

2 tablespoons salted
capers, rinsed of salt

3 to 5 anchovy fillets, rinsed

¼ cup extra-virgin olive oil

Freshly squeezed lemon
juice of ½ lemon

Freshly ground black pepper

Grated Parmigiano-
Reggiano, for garnish

Chopped fresh flat-leaf
parsley, for garnish

1 Place the capers and anchovies in a small pot with the olive oil over medium-low heat, stirring until the anchovies begin to melt. Squeeze the lemon juice over. After arranging the meatballs and the sauce on serving plates, top with black pepper, Parmigiano-Reggiano, and parsley.

fresh tomato sauce

MAKES ABOUT 3 CUPS

THIS IS A SIMPLE SAUCE that cooks up in minutes and is delicious with Fabio's meatballs (page 176), tossed with pasta, on pizza, or warmed and served with fresh mozzarella as a first course.

1 tablespoon extra-virgin olive oil

1 small yellow or white onion, chopped

1 (28-ounce) can crushed San Marzano tomatoes with juices

1 small ripe red tomato, such as Campari or plum, cored and chopped (optional)

2 cloves garlic, chopped

Pinch of dried oregano or Italian seasoning

Sea salt and freshly ground black pepper

Fresh basil leaves, for garnish (optional)

1 Heat the olive oil in a large pot over medium-high heat. Add the onion and cook, stirring occasionally, until soft, about 5 minutes. Add the crushed tomatoes, chopped tomato, if using, garlic, and oregano. Season with salt and pepper to taste. Cook for about 10 minutes. Purée using an immersion blender in the pot, or transfer to a food processor and purée until just blended. Taste and adjust the seasoning as needed. After arranging the meatballs and sauce on serving plates, garnish with fresh basil leaves, if using.

salad of roasted cherries *with* burrata

SERVES 4

I TASTED BURRATA—A FRAGILE, DELICIOUSLY creamy cheese from Puglia made with leftover mozzarella scraps and filled with fresh cream—years ago while traveling in Italy and never thought much about it, probably because almost everything I ate there was singular in its own way. Now, I dream of burrata and eat it whenever I can. Thankfully, it is now widely available in the United States, both in specialty markets and online.

I came across this pairing at Tom Douglas's Serious Pie restaurant in Seattle, and it reminded me of the creamy cheeses that I gorged on when back in Italy. If burrata is not available, substitute a fresh chèvre, fresh ricotta, or the creamiest, freshest mozzarella. If you find yourself wanting this outside of cherry season, substitute thawed frozen cherries. And you can omit the greens, if you wish.

1 pound cherries, pitted

1 teaspoon extra-virgin olive oil, plus more for optional greens and drizzling

8 ounces burrata

2 cups baby kale or arugula (optional)

1 tablespoon balsamic vinegar (optional)

Fleur de sel, Maldon sea salt, or other finishing salt

Fresh mint leaves, for garnish

1 Preheat the oven to 400°F and line a rimmed baking sheet with parchment paper.

2 Toss the cherries with the olive oil and place on the prepared baking sheet. Roast for about 20 minutes. Let cool slightly.

3 Place 2 ounces of burrata per person on each serving plate and place the cherries and juice around the cheese.

4 Toss the baby kale, if using, with 1 to 2 teaspoons of the roasted cherry juice, the balsamic vinegar, if using, and 2 tablespoons olive oil, and mix to combine; serve alongside the cherries and cheese. Sprinkle with fleur de sel, drizzle with olive oil, and garnish with fresh mint.

N O T E : If you find yourself with leftover whole cherry pits (do not use even slightly crushed pits since they are toxic), soak them in red wine or white vinegar overnight, strain, and discard the pits. The resulting vinegar adds both color and a wonderful light fruit flavor to salads, pickles, and more.

roasted cauliflower
with olives and capers

SERVES 6

OLIVES AND CAPERS ARE ABUNDANT in Italian cuisine, and I love them with the crunch of cauliflower. Serve this warm as a side dish, or at room temperature or chilled as a salad. It's also delicious with a fried egg on top for a quick lunch.

1 head cauliflower, cut into small florets

1 cup olives, such as Castelvetrano, Picholine, or Niçoise

1 tablespoon capers, rinsed and drained (coarsely chopped if large)

3½ tablespoons extra-virgin olive oil

Sea salt and freshly ground black pepper

¼ cup chopped shallots

¼ cup golden raisins or dried currants

1 teaspoon Dijon mustard

2 tablespoons freshly squeezed orange juice

1 tablespoon white or red wine vinegar

Fresh flat-leaf parsley leaves or celery leaves, for garnish

1 Preheat the oven to 400°F.

2 Toss the cauliflower, olives, and capers with 2½ tablespoons of the olive oil and sprinkle with salt and black pepper. Spread the cauliflower, capers, and olives evenly on a large shallow rimmed baking sheet and roast for about 20 minutes, until the cauliflower is tender. Tip into a large serving bowl.

3 Combine the shallots, raisins, mustard, orange juice, and vinegar in a small bowl. Gradually whisk in the remaining 1 tablespoon olive oil. Pour the dressing over the cauliflower and toss gently. Taste and add more salt, pepper, or vinegar as needed. Garnish with parsley and serve warm.

one day i, too, can learn the secrets of their wizardry

grilled party pizza

MAKES 6 (8-INCH) PIZZAS

MY FIRST DAY AT FONTE (the mountain house Frances Mayes writes about in *Every Day in Tuscany*), we go for an afternoon swim and then prep for a pizza party, where I find myself in the kitchen with a sweet Italian man named Ivan and his big-hearted, robust mother, Domenica Italiani, who live just up the gravel road at the "House of the Sun." Their faces are like the open sunflowers that brighten the Tuscan hillsides. Together we make pizza dough with flour, a good dose of Bramasole olive oil, salt, and water. No measuring. I've been making pizza for years but realize I've been doing it too precisely. Ivan's method suits me better, for I am a cook who prefers not to measure—who is always tempted by the last-minute handful of this and dash of that.

Ivan, with one hand constantly in motion, gently turns the flour, fresh yeast, and water into a beautiful paste. We knead it, cover it, and let it rise. After an hour or so, I help pinch out moon balls of dough. Mine are not as smooth as Ivan's, but he assures me that they're perfect. "Ohh kay. Very good." He gives me thumbs-up as we toss and turn and flatten the balls to top them with everything from basil, whole sage leaves, and rosemary to caramelized onion, fresh Italian sausage, and mozzarella. Domenica pats my hips and squeezes my arms, tossing flour about me like fairy dust. Ivan and his mother are magicians in the kitchen, and they make me feel that one day I, too, can learn the secrets of their wizardry.

grilled party pizza

CONTINUED

Someone announces the arrival of a whole roasted pig. The porchetta! Kids squeal at the sight of the head—snout, eyes, and all. A Korean-Australian musician arrives, as well as a chef from Los Angeles, a host of North Carolinians, and villagers who have gathered to celebrate twenty years of Frances and Ed here in Cortona—about seventy-five guests in all. A few hours later, Ivan and I take a break and he tells me that we have made sixty-five pizzas in just a few hours. Guests come by to tell us the pizzas were *delizioso*. I am sticky from sweat, the back of my dress covered in Domenica's large, floured handprints. What a *brava ragazza* you are, Ivan keeps telling me. No sleep and sixty-five pizzas. *Brava. Brava.*

This is my version of that pizza, grilled, in memory of that festive occasion. This yields a lovely, tender, thin crust. In Italy, they use a fine "oo" flour, but bread flour or all-purpose flour is also good. Gather all your toppings and let guests create their own pizza flavor combinations.

DOUGH

1 (¼-ounce) package active dry yeast

1¼ cups warm water (about 110°F)

1 teaspoon honey or sugar, plus a pinch if needed

3 tablespoons olive oil

2 teaspoons salt

3½ to 4 cups bread flour (you can also use "oo" or all-purpose)

Cornmeal, as needed

TOPPING POSSIBILITIES

Olive oil

Tomato sauce

Thinly sliced yellow onion, mushroom, or tomato

Fresh herbs, such as basil, flat-leaf parsley, and mint

Nduja or other spreadable salami

Thin slices of prosciutto di Parma or pepperoni

Mascarpone

Shredded or crumbled mozzarella, feta, Parmigiano-Reggiano, Fontina, smoked provolone, or other cheese

Eggs

1 To make the dough, in the bowl of a stand mixer, sprinkle the yeast over the warm water and let stand for about 5 minutes, until frothy. If it doesn't froth, add a pinch of sugar; if it still doesn't froth, start over with new yeast. Stir in the olive oil, salt, and sugar. Using the paddle attachment, slowly add 3½ cups of the flour and mix for about 1 minute. Switch to the dough hook and knead on medium-low speed for 8 minutes. If the dough is sticking a bit to the bottom of the bowl, add a bit more flour. Alternatively, you can use a large bowl and make the dough by hand. Let the yeast proof the same way, and mix in the flour with a large spoon. When ready to knead, turn the dough out onto a lightly floured surface. Knead it by hand until the dough is smooth and elastic, 8 to 10 minutes.

2 Coat a large bowl with about a tablespoon of oil. Place the dough in the bowl and turn to coat all sides with oil. Cover with a clean kitchen towel or plastic wrap, place in a warm spot, and let rise for about 1 hour. (The dough can be made ahead; freeze the dough in an airtight container for up to 1 week.)

3 Heat a grill to about 450°F and oil the grill grates. Punch down the dough and roll out on a floured surface to about an 8-inch round. You will probably have to grill the pizzas in batches. Scatter some cornmeal on a pizza peel or rimless baking sheet or cutting board. Place the rolled-out dough on top of the cornmeal. Gently slide the dough off the peel and onto the hot grill. Cover with the lid and grill for about 2 minutes. The bottom of the dough should start to turn dark golden brown but not black. If it's still not browning, increase the heat; it should only take about 2 minutes.

4 Slide the dough back onto the peel; flip over so that the cooked side faces up. Drizzle with olive oil and a light layer of tomato sauce, if using, and scatter the other toppings over, ending with the cheese. Remember to keep the toppings light so that the pizza doesn't get soggy or too heavy. Gently slide the pizza back onto the grill. If you like, crack an egg on top in the center of the pizza. Cover with the grill lid and decrease the heat to about 400°F. Grill for about 5 minutes, or until the dough is cooked and golden and the topping is bubbling and melted. Check the pizza and make sure the crust is not burning on the bottom. If so, decrease the heat. Transfer the pizza from the grill to a cutting board; let rest for a few minutes before cutting.

pici *with* popped tomatoes, anchovies, and onions

SERVES 2

PICI, A THICK, SOFT, EGGLESS hand-rolled pasta similar to fat spaghetti, is a classic Tuscan offering. I had a delicious version at a small pizzeria in Cortona, where Frances and Ed would take us after we had cooked our hearts out and, on rare occasion, couldn't muster dinner.

The simplicity of the sauce—fresh tomato, garlic, dried chile flakes, and olive oil—makes the pasta shine. I've added anchovy and olives. Substitute penne, spaghetti, or bigoli.

3 tablespoons extra-virgin olive oil

3 cloves garlic, thinly sliced

4 to 5 anchovy fillets

A handful of black olives (such as Niçoise or Kalamata)

Red pepper flakes

2 cups cherry or grape tomatoes, finely chopped

Sea salt and freshly ground black pepper

8 ounces pici

Grated Parmigiano-Reggiano or Pecorino Romano, for garnish

1 Heat the olive oil in a large skillet over medium heat. Add the garlic and swirl the pan to flavor the oil, about 1 minute. Add the anchovies, olives, and red pepper flakes and toss to combine. Add the tomatoes and cook, tossing often, for about 5 minutes. Season with salt and pepper to taste. Lower the heat.

2 Cook the pasta in salted boiling water just until al dente. Drain, reserving about ¼ cup of the pasta cooking water. Add the cooked pasta to the skillet with the tomatoes. Toss and heat for about 1 minute, adding some of the reserved pasta water if too dry. Toss to combine. Serve immediately, garnished with another crack of black pepper and cheese.

i went back the next day . . . and then back again a third time just to make sure i hadn't imagined it all

vanilla bean panna cotta

SERVES 8

THE FIRST TIME I TASTED PANNA COTTA was in Florence in the early 1990s at a restaurant whose name I no longer recall; I just remember that I was smitten with its quivering center and the accompanying dark chocolate sauce. I went back the next day for a different version, with fresh red fruit coulis, and then back again a third time just to make sure I hadn't imagined it all. Now, panna cotta is on many restaurant menus here in the United States as well as in Europe, and inevitably I've run into disappointing versions that are often rubbery with too much gelatin.

I like it silky and when it jiggles just so. I've made this with buttermilk, almond milk, yogurt, and heavy cream; experiment and come up with your favorite ingredient and flavor combination. A perfect panna cotta needs only a spoon, but there are endless ways to gussy it up. Try a citrus marmalade, a warm, deep, dark chocolate sauce, fresh fruit whizzed up in the blender, or even some berries and a dash of thick, aged balsamico.

Butter or neutral-flavored oil, for the ramekins (optional)

1 cup whole milk

2 teaspoons unflavored powdered gelatin

2½ cups heavy cream

½ cup sugar

½ vanilla bean, split lengthwise

1 Gather 8 small (about 4-ounce) ramekins, glass bowls, or coffee cups. (If unmolding your panna cotta onto plates, you can grease the inside of these with a little butter or neutral-flavored oil for easier unmolding.)

2 Pour ½ cup of the milk into a small bowl and sprinkle the gelatin over. Let dissolve for 10 to 15 minutes.

3 Combine the cream, sugar, and the remaining ½ cup milk in a medium saucepan over medium-high heat. Scrape the seeds from the vanilla bean into the pot, and add the pod. Bring to a simmer and stir until the sugar dissolves. Remove the pan from the heat and let the vanilla steep for about 10 minutes.

4 Remove the pod and bring the mixture back to a simmer; stir in the gelatin-milk mixture and stir until dissolved, 2 to 3 minutes. Strain the mixture through a fine-mesh sieve into the ramekins. Chill for at least 6 hours before serving. If you would like to unmold them, run a sharp knife around the edge of each ramekin and dip the bottom in warm water to help release the panna cotta.

Golden Brioche,
page 193

where everyone wants confirmation that you will
... always come back to grace their tables

almond milk granita

MAKES 3 CUPS

IN FLORENCE, THERE ARE a number of excellent places to satisfy a gelato craving, but my favorite is Carabé, near the Accademia Gallery. The first time I tasted anything from this Sicilian-style gelateria, it was 4 P.M. and I was departing the next morning. After one bite of almond granita and upon hearing that they closed at 7 P.M., I walked around the Duomo, returned for another serving, walked around again, and came back for one more bite.

The next time I visited, I met owner Antonio Lisciandro, who was eager to have me taste as many flavors as possible. I was in heaven but so animated with the tasting frenzy that I ended up twisting my ankle. "Sit," Antonio told me as he packed some gelato into plastic wrap and placed it on my quickly swelling ankle. As I contemplated the difference between the healing powers of gelato versus a pack of frozen peas, he asked me why I didn't just move to Florence. A good question and one worth pondering. "You will come back to visit, yes?" he asked. Yes, I nodded, how could I not return to a place where someone will feed me endless spoonfuls of granita and gently ice down my ankle with handmade gelato? "You will come back," he said again, but it wasn't really a question.

almond milk granita

CONTINUED

Florence, I've learned over the years and many visits, is a city of affirmatives. A city of return, a place where everyone wants confirmation that you will love their produce, shop their markets, visit their galleries, and always come back to grace their tables.

For this granita, I don't peel my almonds, but if you prefer skinless, peel yours. Serve as is or as they do in Sicily, stuffed into a brioche (page 193), and chase with a strong espresso.

1½ cups whole almonds

1 cup confectioners' sugar

2¼ cups spring water (not carbonated)

1 Blend the almonds, sugar, and 1¾ cups of the spring water in a blender or food processor until smooth and foamy. Pour the almond mixture through a fine-mesh sieve into a loaf pan or freezer-safe square baking pan. Add the remaining ½ cup spring water to the solids in the sieve and whisk over the almond mixture so that most of the water passes through and into the pan. Discard any remaining solids (or blend in a glass with a bit of milk and enjoy). Stir the mixture and place in the freezer. Scrape with a fork every 30 minutes, crushing any large solid pieces, until firm but not completely frozen, about 2 hours. Scrape again with a fork before serving. This is best eaten the day it's made. Let it soften a bit before serving.

golden brioche

SERVES 6

MY IDEAL BREAKFAST SANDWICH is inspired by summer breakfasts down in Sicily, where they bake up *brioscia col tuppo*, small brioche buns often served for breakfast stuffed with gelato or granita. This makes 6 buns in a single loaf pan.

Scant ⅓ cup warm whole milk (about 110°F)

1 (¼-ounce) package active dry yeast

2 tablespoons fine sugar

¾ teaspoon fine sea salt, plus a pinch for the egg wash

2 cups unbleached all-purpose flour

2 large eggs, at room temperature

½ cup (1 stick) unsalted butter, softened and cut into 8 pieces

1 egg yolk

1 Combine the warm milk, yeast, sugar, and the ¾ teaspoon salt in the bowl of a stand mixer fitted with the paddle attachment and stir with a spoon. Let sit for 10 minutes, or until the mixture is frothy. Mix on low speed, slowly adding the flour and mixing until well-combined. Add the eggs, one at a time, and mix on low speed until combined. Change the paddle for the dough hook and mix on medium speed for about 2 minutes. Scrape down the sides of the bowl and continue to mix for another 2 to 3 minutes, until the dough is smooth. If the dough sticks to the hook, scrape the dough off into the bowl.

2 Add 4 pieces of the butter, 2 at a time, and mix on medium-low speed until incorporated; scrape the dough off the hook as needed. Add the remaining 4 pieces butter, a piece at a time, while mixing, until each piece is well-incorporated. Increase the speed to medium and mix until the dough is smooth and elastic again, 3 to 4 minutes. Stop and scrape the dough hook, sides, and bottom of the bowl as needed. Mix again at medium speed until the dough is smooth and shiny. The dough will be very moist, especially if your kitchen is warm, but try not to add more flour or the brioche might turn out tough.

golden brioche

3 Place the dough on a very lightly floured surface and knead a few times, folding the dough over and onto itself a few times. Make a ball, tucking the underside of the dough to form a smooth top. Transfer the dough, smooth side up, to a large bowl, cover with plastic wrap, and let rise in a warm, draft-free spot for 2 hours. Or, let rise for 1 hour, turn the dough out onto a clean surface, and knead a few times, then form a ball again and place back in the bowl; cover tightly with plastic wrap and let rise in the refrigerator overnight.

4 If the dough was refrigerated, bring the dough to room temperature. Butter an 8- or 9-inch loaf pan. Turn the dough out onto a clean work surface; cut into 6 equal pieces and form each into a ball. Place the balls in the pan; it's okay if they touch one another. Cover loosely with plastic wrap and let rise for about 1 hour, or until almost doubled in size. Meanwhile, preheat the oven to 375°F and place an oven rack in the center of the oven.

5 Beat the egg yolk with the pinch of salt. Lightly brush the top of the brioche with the egg wash, making sure not to get any on the sides so the loaf does not stick to the pan. Using scissors, snip the dough at the top of each ball. Or, pinch some of the dough from each large ball and make smaller balls and place on top (as in photo). Bake for 10 minutes. Decrease the heat to 350°F and bake for another 10 to 12 minutes, until the loaf is cooked on the inside and golden brown on top and lightly golden on the sides. Let cool in the pan on a cooling rack for about 5 minutes before unmolding.

Almond Milk Granita,
page 191

lagniappe

an orphan's thanksgiving

DURING THE TEN YEARS or so when I lived in Europe, I rarely made it back to the United States for Thanksgiving, but it is my favorite food holiday. So I have learned to celebrate the occasion wherever I happen to be—Sweden, Provence, a Paris bistro, and more recently in snowy Alaska. Over the years, I've always seemed to find a group of new and old friends who aren't going "home" for the holidays. As the head orphan, it's my duty to orchestrate a memorable meal. The menus change as cities and landscapes vary, and everyone contributes something new. Some tables have been laden with kimchi fried rice next to Swedish potato and salmon pudding. Or with turkey "in mourning" (a whole turkey covered in a layer of thinly sliced black truffle tucked under the skin) making nice with cheesy mashed potatoes and string bean casserole.

The dressings and sides often favor corn bread (bless the hearts of the die-hard Southerners in the group) and oyster (my grandfather's favorite), winter greens, and creamy baked gratins. Gravy is sometimes fortified with Madeira or Port. And usually the best bakers among us bring all manner of desserts, from traditional pies of pumpkin and pecan to sweet potato flan, boozy whiskey ice cream, and sponge cake trifles plump with cream and fruit filling so divine I always mean to set some aside to savor later, chilled, preferably wearing looser pants and the softest T-shirt I can find.

If dessert proves too much, sometimes a simple platter of cheeses and Medjool dates, or a bowl of bright orange clementines and rosy pomegranates, will do the trick. Or a lighter fruit-laced treat like Vanilla Custard–Filled Baked Apples (page 213) or Fresh Pear Cake with Almonds (page 86).

salad of brussels sprouts and kale with pear *and* pomegranate

SERVES 6

EXACT RECIPES FOR SALADS are almost futile because so much depends on what Mother Nature has made available. The most important thing about this salad is to very thinly slice the Brussels sprouts and the kale. The rest is really improv and depends on what you feel like tossing in. Sometimes I like these greens with a bit more sass and will add garlic and anchovy, or sometimes I will smooth things out with a Southern-inspired buttermilk-herb dressing.

SHALLOT VINAIGRETTE

MAKES ABOUT ½ CUP

1 tablespoon minced shallot

1½ tablespoons freshly squeezed lemon juice (preferably Meyer lemon)

1 tablespoon champagne vinegar, red wine vinegar, or balsamic vinegar

1 teaspoon Dijon mustard

⅛ teaspoon fine sea salt

¼ cup extra-virgin olive oil

SALAD

8 ounces Brussels sprouts (about 12 sprouts), cored, halved, and very thinly sliced

1 (8-ounce) bunch kale, thinly sliced

1 tablespoon fresh squeezed lemon juice

Salt, preferably fleur de sel or Maldon sea salt

1 ripe but firm pear, cored and thinly sliced

2 to 3 tablespoons torn fresh herbs, such as flat-leaf parsley, dill, chives, or your choice

1 small clove garlic, minced (optional)

Freshly ground black pepper

⅓ to ½ cup walnut halves or pine nuts, toasted

Arils from ½ pomegranate

Shavings of Parmigiano-Reggiano or ricotta salata (optional)

CONTINUED

salad of brussels sprouts and kale with pear *and* pomegranate

CONTINUED

1 To make the vinaigrette, combine the shallot, lemon juice, vinegar, mustard, and salt in a small bowl. Slowly whisk in the olive oil until well-combined.

2 To make the salad, toss the Brussels sprouts and kale together in a large bowl with the lemon juice and a pinch of salt; massage the sprouts and kale with the juice and salt to soften the leaves. Add the pear, herbs, and garlic, if using, together in a large salad bowl. Toss with the vinaigrette. Taste and add more salt and pepper as needed. Add the nuts, pomegranate arils, and cheese shavings. Serve at once. If you want to make it ahead, keep the salad cool and toss with the dressing, nuts, and cheese just before serving.

radish and pink lady apple salad *with* fennel and mint

SERVES 6 TO 8

THIS SIMPLE YET ELEGANT fall salad, inspired by autumn markets, is best spread out on a shallow platter for all the ingredients to show off their shape and color. Use a mandoline slicer for even, paper-thin slices. And toss in fresh tarragon or chervil along with, or in place of, the mint. Sometimes I add blood orange or satsuma sections for sweetness and color.

4 to 6 French breakfast or other radishes, trimmed and thinly sliced

2 crisp sweet-tart apples (such as Pink Lady or Gala), cored, halved, and thinly sliced

1 small fennel bulb, trimmed and thinly sliced

1 to 2 tablespoons freshly squeezed lemon juice (preferably Meyer lemon)

1 cup tightly packed celery leaves

2 to 3 tablespoons chopped fresh mint

High-quality extra-virgin olive oil, such as Bramasole olive oil, for drizzling

Fleur de sel or Maldon sea salt

Walnuts or hazelnuts toasted, for garnish

1 Toss the radishes, apples, and fennel in a large bowl with the lemon juice. Add the celery leaves and mint. Arrange on a platter. Drizzle liberally with olive oil; sprinkle with salt and more lemon juice to taste. Garnish with toasted nuts and serve.

as the head orphan, it's my duty to orchestrate a memorable meal

the menus change as cities and landscapes vary, and everyone contributes something new

poppy's oyster dressing

SERVES 8

EVERY THANKSGIVING WHEN I was growing up, my whole
family looked forward to my grandfather's Gulf oyster dressing more
than anything else, even the pies. Sometimes, Poppy would pile this
spicy, oyster-laden goodness onto pork chops before baking and
smothering them in gravy. Leftover
dressing is a must on turkey
sandwiches the next day.

4½ cups cubed white bread, such as baguette (preferably day-old; 8 ounces)

1½ cups milk or water

2 tablespoons olive oil

1 cup chopped white or yellow onion

½ cup chopped celery

3 to 4 cloves garlic, chopped

2 teaspoons dried Italian seasoning or herbes de Provence

¾ teaspoon fine sea salt

¼ teaspoon freshly ground black pepper

¼ teaspoon cayenne pepper

2 pints shucked oysters, plus the liquor of only 1 pint, pulsed 8 to 10 times in a food processor

Juice of 1 lemon

1 cup dry bread crumbs

3 green onions, finely chopped

2 to 3 tablespoons chopped fresh flat-leaf parsley

¼ cup finely grated Parmigiano-Reggiano

1 tablespoon unsalted butter, cut into 9 pieces

1 Place the cubed bread in a bowl, pour the milk over, and let the bread soak while you proceed with step 2. Meanwhile, preheat the oven to 350°F.

2 Heat the oil in a large skillet (a heavy-bottomed cast-iron skillet is best) over medium-high heat. Add the onion, celery; stir in the garlic, Italian seasoning, salt, black pepper, and cayenne; stir to combine, and cook for about 7 minutes, or until the vegetables are tender.

3 Remove the bread from the bowl, squeezing the milk out of the bread; discard the milk. Add the bread to the vegetables and cook over medium-high heat, scraping the bottom of the pan if the bread sticks, until the bread is golden and no longer wet, about 5 minutes. Add the puréed oysters with the liquor; stir to combine. Add the lemon juice, bread crumbs, green onions, and parsley; stir and cook until the oysters begin to curl but do not cook completely, about 2 minutes. Turn off the heat. The dressing will be moist, on the wetter side, but it will dry out a bit as it bakes. Taste and add more salt, pepper, or lemon juice as needed.

4 Spoon the dressing into a 9-inch square or 10-inch round baking dish that's at least 2 inches deep. Sprinkle evenly with the Parmigiano-Reggiano and dot with the butter pieces. Bake uncovered for 30 to 40 minutes, until golden and bubbling on top.

Salad of Brussels Sprouts and Kale with Pear and Pomegranate, page 199; Roasted Squash with Mint and Hazelnuts, page 210; Cranberry-Tangerine-Ginger Compote, page 209.

roast turkey with pancetta, kumquats, and prunes

SERVES 10 TO 12

I HAVE COOKED MANY TURKEYS over the years using many flavor combinations. In some countries, turkeys just don't elicit the same feelings of goodwill and memories of memorable meals that they do for us in the United States. This is my go-to because it has been a crowd-pleaser for all different palates. I like the contrast of prunes and fresh citrus with the salty chunks of pancetta, not to mention how it helps a tough old bird triumph in the face of so much anticipation. Kumquats add bursts of color and flavor to the traditional turkey and are worth seeking out; otherwise, substitute small clementines or mandarinquats.

HERB BUTTER

MAKES ½ CUP

½ cup (1 stick) salted butter

2 cloves garlic, peeled

½ cup tightly packed combination of fresh herbs, such as rosemary, parsley, and sage

¼ teaspoon freshly ground black pepper

TURKEY

1 (12- to 14-pound) pound turkey, thawed if frozen

Sea salt and freshly ground black pepper

1 small yellow or white onion, quartered

4 to 6 cloves garlic

1 lemon, halved

4 to 5 thyme sprigs

1 cup (2 sticks) salted butter, melted

1 (11-ounce) slab thick-cut pancetta, cut into ½-inch chunks

14 to 16 kumquats or 8 small clementines, halved

18 to 20 pitted prunes

1 cup dry red or white wine

2 to 3 cups chicken stock

CONTINUED

roast turkey with pancetta, kumquats, and prunes

CONTINUED

1 Preheat the oven to 400°F and place an oven rack on the lowest level of the oven.

2 To make the herb butter, combine all of the ingredients in a food processor and blend until just combined.

3 Remove the innards from the turkey and rinse the turkey inside and out. Dry with paper towels. Season the turkey inside and out generously with salt and pepper; stuff the cavity with the onion, garlic, lemon, and thyme sprigs. Rub the herb butter under the skin of the turkey, trying not to pierce the skin, to cover the breast and thigh meat. Rub the turkey all over with the melted butter. Tie the legs together and tuck the wings under the bird. Place the turkey breast side down on a roasting rack in a roasting pan. Roast in the oven for 30 minutes.

4 Remove the pan from the oven and carefully turn the turkey over, so that the breast side is up, protecting your hands with oven mitts or kitchen towels. Decrease the oven temperature to 350°F, return the turkey to the oven, and let cook for 45 minutes.

5 Remove the pan and add the pancetta, kumquats, and prunes to the bottom of the pan; place the turkey back in the oven. Let cook until an instant-read thermometer inserted in the breast without touching bone registers 160°F (the turkey will continue to cook and the internal temperature will rise another 5 to 10 degrees), another 1 hour and 15 minutes to 1 hour and 30 minutes). If desired, baste with the pan juices every 30 minutes, preferably without removing the turkey from the oven and as quickly as possible.

6 When the turkey is done, remove the pan from the oven and tilt the turkey so the juices from the cavity run into the pan. Transfer the turkey to a cutting board, tent loosely with aluminum foil, and let sit for at least 20 minutes.

7 Make the gravy by removing the pancetta, kumquats, and prunes from the pan; reserve and keep warm. Gently pour the pan juices into a glass measuring cup or fat separator; let the fat rise to the top and skim off the fat and discard. Reserve the juices. Place the roasting pan over medium-high heat, add the wine, and stir, scraping brown bits from the bottom of the pan. Bring to a boil, and then add the chicken stock and cook until reduced by half. Add the skimmed pan juices and cook for a few minutes more. Strain into a gravy boat.

8 Carve the turkey and serve with the reserved pancetta, kumquats, and prunes on the side.

cranberry-tangerine-ginger compote

MAKES ABOUT 4 CUPS

CANNED CRANBERRY jelly with the ridges has its place and often brings back fond memories of childhood holiday meals, but this is a fresh, tart alternative that also incorporates winter citrus. This compote is also delicious with roast pork or chicken, layered into a sponge cake, or as a condiment for leftover turkey sandwiches. Because you are not peeling the citrus, it's best to use organic fruit for this dish.

3 small tangerines, clementines, or kumquats

1 cup sugar

½ cup freshly squeezed orange juice

12 ounces to 1 pound fresh or thawed frozen cranberries

1 teaspoon grated fresh ginger

1 whole star anise

1 cinnamon stick

1 Wash the tangerines thoroughly and cut crosswise and then into quarters (if using kumquats, you will only need to halve them). Combine the tangerines with the sugar and orange juice in a medium pot over medium-high heat and cook until the sugar dissolves. Decrease the heat and let simmer, stirring occasionally, for about 30 minutes, or until the tangerine skins are soft and the liquid is syrupy.

2 Turn the heat to medium and stir in the cranberries, ginger, star anise, and cinnamon; cook for about 10 minutes, or until the cranberry skins just begin to split. Let cool, then chill until ready to serve. The compote will keep, stored in the refrigerator, for up to 1 week.

roasted squash
with mint and hazelnuts

SERVES 6 TO 8

AUTUMNAL SQUASH ADDS SO MUCH texture, color, and flavor to the holiday table that I always include it in some way, whether in a pie, soufflé, or salad. Toasted hazelnut oil works well with this dish. Chopped toasted pistachios or walnuts with the corresponding oil would be fine substitutes. La Tourangelle makes excellent nut oils, which can be found in specialty food shops and many supermarkets.

3 medium acorn or butternut squash

2½ tablespoons extra-virgin olive oil

Sea salt and freshly ground black pepper

½ cup chopped toasted hazelnuts

Hazelnut oil, for drizzling

Fresh mint leaves, for garnish

Fresh pomegranate arils or toasted pumpkin seeds, for garnish (optional)

1 Preheat the oven to 425°F.

2 Cut the squash in half lengthwise and scrape out the seeds and strings using a large spoon. Cut each half into 2-inch wedges, leaving the skin on. Toss the wedges with the olive oil and season with salt and pepper. Place the wedges, cut side down, on a large rimmed baking sheet. Roast for 25 to 30 minutes, turning halfway through, until golden on both sides.

3 Arrange on a platter, drizzle with hazelnut oil, and garnish with mint leaves. Sprinkle fresh pomegranate arils or toasted pumpkin seeds, if using, over the top and serve.

vanilla custard–filled baked apples

SERVES 6

HOLIDAY DESSERTS RUN THE GAMUT from sticky-sweet pies to sugar-laden cakes. I like offering fruit as an alternative, and for me, there's nothing more comforting than a soft baked apple. Delicious on their own, but paired with this custard sauce, the apples make for a humble yet remarkable addition to any festive occasion. The custard sauce is also good to serve with cakes and pies. If you prefer to make only the apples, serve them with freshly whipped cream or vanilla ice cream.

VANILLA CUSTARD SAUCE

MAKES ABOUT 2½ CUPS

1¼ cups heavy cream

1 cup whole milk or half-and-half

1 vanilla bean, halved lengthwise

6 egg yolks

⅓ cup sugar

BAKED APPLES

6 medium Granny Smith or Golden Delicious apples

Light brown sugar, as needed

3 tablespoons unsalted butter

Freshly squeezed lemon juice, as needed

Ground cinnamon, for sprinkling (optional)

1 To make the custard sauce, combine the cream and milk in a medium saucepan. Scrape the vanilla seeds into the milk mixture and add the pod to the pan. Bring the milk to a low boil; turn off the heat and let the vanilla steep in the warm milk mixture while making the rest of the custard.

2 Place the egg yolks and sugar in a medium bowl; whisk vigorously for a minute or so, until the mixture turns thick and pale yellow. Remove the vanilla pod from the milk mixture and gradually add the hot milk to the yolk mixture, whisking constantly. Return the mixture to the saucepan and stir over medium heat (do not let boil) for about 3 minutes, until the custard thickens slightly and coats the back of a wooden spoon. It will thicken more as it cools. The final consistency should be that of heavy cream. Remove from the heat and strain through a fine-mesh sieve into a bowl. Chill until ready to serve.

3 To make the apples, preheat the oven to 350°F. Butter a baking dish large enough to hold the number of apples you're making.

CONTINUED

vanilla custard–filled baked apples

CONTINUED

4 Core the apples all the way through. Place in the dish, taking care so the apples do
   not touch (otherwise they will stick together when baked). If the apples are wobbly,
   trim a slice off the very bottom so they stand up evenly. Score the apples, using a
   knife point, about ½ inch down from the top, all the way around the apple. This
   will help keep the apple skins from bursting. Fill each cored center with brown
   sugar and 1½ teaspoons of butter. Squeeze lemon juice all over and sprinkle with
   cinnamon, if using. Bake for 40 to 50 minutes, until the apples are puffed and the
   center is tender when pierced with a knife. Some of the skins might burst, but not
   to worry, especially once you pour the custard sauce over. Serve the apples with
   the sauce poured on top and more served on the side.

goodbye to all that
—for neil

1.

I'm here to say goodbye
so that when you, somewhere in the very near future, will be with me
and I with you, I will be ready.

To prepare myself, I ride through the city streets with all the windows down
and eat strategically—sitting at counters in the off hours
in the off chance I might be able
to put something delicious in my mouth
and think of you

the man I have not yet met
but who is waiting.
To ready myself
I must first join the poet
on a midtown rooftop for bourbon and prosecco
and discuss the business of happiness
convince him/convince myself that I have decided to accept it.
But, I say: Who wants to rush into happiness?
We have to be careful because it could be for the rest of our lives.

Then tepid tea with the musician-turned-hedge-fund-manager
who now also has a wife and three young boys.
He tells me it is killing him
to know I am here in his city and not with him.
He follows me on Twitter and knows every crumb
I leave behind.

All of this in preparation for the man I will love
who plans trips for me to places
where the oysters are cold and sweet
and the bakeries filled pre-dawn
full of flour, water, and salt
that will warm and fill my mouth.

II.

I'm here to say hello
to greet this newness of belonging
a new definition of family
one in which I am no longer on the outside
looking in.

Why this need to record
the beginning of whatever this is . . .
in case we mis-under-stand?
I think out loud: I want to be anchored.
You respond: I want to be more.

So here are the things I will do for you:
Make fresh cucumber ginger juice,
knead dough and make fresh pizza with your family.
And I will watch over you in the quiet of the night
while you dream me near
and wonder how did all the paths lead to here
to this country, to this balcony overlooking
lilac trees and mountains aflame with sun at midnight.

Sometimes I might be distant, and turn far far away
because I will have to step outside
of myself in order not to forget
what it was like
(before you, before this)

And if you reach for me
in the pre-light, maybe just this once
I will finally believe the words others have said
but that you mean:
I am your home.
We are your family.

Tuck me into you
let me rest there for I am tired
of never letting go.
This time
you will not have to explain when I hear you whisper
You are here.

menu ideas

metric conversions *and* equivalents

APPROXIMATE METRIC EQUIVALENTS

VOLUME

¼ teaspoon	1 milliliter
½ teaspoon	2.5 milliliters
¾ teaspoon	4 milliliters
1 teaspoon	5 milliliters
1¼ teaspoons	6 milliliters
1½ teaspoons	7.5 milliliters
1¾ teaspoons	8.5 milliliters
2 teaspoons	10 milliliters
1 tablespoon (½ fluid ounce)	15 milliliters
2 tablespoons (1 fluid ounce)	30 milliliters
¼ cup	60 milliliters
⅓ cup	80 milliliters
½ cup (4 fluid ounces)	120 milliliters
⅔ cup	160 milliliters
¾ cup	180 milliliters
1 cup (8 fluid ounces)	240 milliliters
1¼ cups	300 milliliters
1½ cups (12 fluid ounces)	360 milliliters
1⅔ cups	400 milliliters
2 cups (1 pint)	460 milliliters
3 cups	700 milliliters
4 cups (1 quart)	0.95 liter
1 quart plus ¼ cup	1 liter
4 quarts (1 gallon)	3.8 liters

LENGTH

⅛ inch	3 millimeters
¼ inch	6 millimeters
½ inch	1¼ centimeters
1 inch	2½ centimeters
2 inches	5 centimeters
2½ inches	6 centimeters
4 inches	10 centimeters
5 inches	13 centimeters
6 inches	15¼ centimeters
12 inches (1 foot)	30 centimeters

WEIGHT

¼ ounce	7 grams
½ ounce	14 grams
¾ ounce	21 grams
1 ounce	28 grams
1¼ ounces	35 grams
1½ ounces	42.5 grams
1⅔ ounces	45 grams
2 ounces	57 grams
3 ounces	85 grams
4 ounces (¼ pound)	113 grams
5 ounces	142 grams
6 ounces	170 grams
7 ounces	198 grams
8 ounces (½ pound)	227 grams
16 ounces (1 pound)	454 grams
35.25 ounces (2.2 pounds)	1 kilogram

METRIC CONVERSION FORMULAS

TO CONVERT	MULTIPLY
Ounces to grams	Ounces by 28.35
Pounds to kilograms	Pounds by .454
Teaspoons to milliliters	Teaspoons by 4.93
Tablespoons to milliliters	Tablespoons by 14.79
Fluid ounces to milliliters	Fluid ounces by 29.57
Cups to milliliters	Cups by 236.59
Cups to liters	Cups by .236
Pints to liters	Pints by .473
Quarts to liters	Quarts by .946
Gallons to liters	Gallons by 3.785
Inches to centimeters	Inches by 2.54

COMMON INGREDIENTS AND THEIR APPROXIMATE EQUIVALENTS

1 cup uncooked white rice = 185 grams

1 cup all-purpose flour = 140 grams

1 stick butter (4 ounces • ½ cup • 8 tablespoons) = 110 grams

1 cup butter (8 ounces • 2 sticks • 16 tablespoons) = 220 grams

1 cup brown sugar, firmly packed = 225 grams

1 cup granulated sugar = 200 grams

OVEN TEMPERATURES

To convert Fahrenheit to Celsius, subtract 32 from Fahrenheit, multiply the result by 5, then divide by 9.

DESCRIPTION	FAHRENHEIT	CELSIUS	BRITISH GAS MARK
Very cool	200°	95°	0
Very cool	225°	110°	¼
Very cool	250°	120°	½
Cool	275°	135°	1
Cool	300°	150°	2
Warm	325°	165°	3
Moderate	350°	175°	4
Moderately hot	375°	190°	5
Fairly hot	400°	200°	6
Hot	425°	220°	7
Very hot	450°	230°	8
Very hot	475°	245°	9

Information compiled from a variety of sources, including *Recipes into Type* by Joan Whitman and Dolores Simon (Newton, MA: Biscuit Books, 2000); *The New Food Lover's Companion* by Sharon Tyler Herbst (Hauppauge, NY: Barron's, 1995); and *Rosemary Brown's Big Kitchen Instruction Book* (Kansas City, MO: Andrews McMeel, 1998).

index